OCCUPATION DIARIES

RAJA SHEHADEH

P
PROFILE BOOKS

First published in Great Britain in 2012 by
PROFILE BOOKS LTD
3A Exmouth House
Pine Street
London EC1R 0JH
www.profilebooks.com

1 3 5 7 9 10 8 6 4 2

Typeset in Aldus by MacGuru Ltd
info@macguru.org.uk
Printed and bound in Great Britain by
Clays, Bungay, Suffolk

The moral right of the author has been asserted.

A CIP catalogue record for this book is available from the
British Library.

ISBN 978 1 78125 016 7
eISBN 978 1 84765 852 4

The paper this book is printed on is certified by the © 1996 Forest
Stewardship Council A.C. (FSC). It is ancient-forest friendly. The
printer holds FSC chain of custody SGS-COC-2061

FSC
Mixed Sources
Product group from well-managed
forests and other controlled sources
Cert no. SGS-COC-2061
www.fsc.org
© 1996 Forest Stewardship Council

To Leonard Woolf, who answered Virginia upon being called to listen to Hitler on the radio: 'I shan't come. I'm planting iris, which will be flowering long after Hitler is gone.'

The variety of wild flowers in the Palestinian countryside even with the scant rainfall is astounding.

I'm just back from a lovely day spent in Wadi Qelt, the ravine on the way between Jerusalem and Jericho. This is one of the few places in the West Bank where you can be sure of finding water even after the drought of the past eight months.

I was with a mixed group of Palestinians and foreigners, photographers and teachers, all of us living and working in the West Bank. Turned out we were not the only ones who had had the idea of an outing there. Just after we put down our rucksacks and stretched out on the rock in the sun a Palestinian family of nine arrived. They were disappointed to find us there but settled for the second-best slab of rock on the opposite side of the pool. Their smaller group comprised two bearded men, two young women with the *hijab* (headscarf) and another of indeterminate age with the *niqab* (face-cover), and four children. All the women wore long black skirts. As soon as I saw them I wondered how they had managed the rocky path without falling in the water. The women in our group invariably wore jeans and colourful shirts.

I had been thinking as we passed the Israeli checkpoint of how clothes distinguish the various groups in our tiny land. The female Israeli soldiers wore tight khaki trousers, the low waist emphasizing the contours of their hips, and were bedecked with mobile phones. They looked at us through their dark sunglasses, giving orders with their hands while exchanging flirty looks and sexual innuendoes with the male soldiers, with whom they conversed in loud Hebrew. To them we were mere specks on the terrain that belonged exclusively to them and they could move us around with a flick of their little finger like pieces on a chequerboard. They lived in their own world, operating the highly technical security apparatus that they seemed to believe entitled them to an exclusive place in the advanced western world.

From the way we appeared and dressed, the sombre-looking family must have suspected that we were Israelis. But there was only a short distance between us. The ravine we were in was deep, with high rock walls bordering it and a pool of water between the slabs on which we spread out that was fed by cascading water from the Fawwar spring, so called because of its sporadic flow. Our fellow picnickers were within earshot and could easily hear us speaking Arabic, so they must soon have realized the nationality of most members of our group. Unfortunately, we did not do what would have been normal a few years ago, perhaps because we drew an imaginary line between us, with them, the suspected Islamists, on one side and us seculars on the other, with the water in between. No one from our side either greeted them or went over to their side to invite them to join us on our rock, which was large enough to accommodate them as well. So a distance was established between us from the beginning, much wider than the natural divide, the small pool of water that separated us.

We spread a red and white checked cloth over the rock and placed on it the different salads and vegetable dishes we had brought with us. We ended with a colourful display, all entirely vegetarian. There was beetroot salad, *baba ganoush* [an aubergine dip], goat's cheese, a bowl of carrots, tomatoes and broccoli, different kinds of patties and fruits. As we settled down to eat, the men from the group opposite left the women and children to search for dry wood for their barbecue of *kufta* and lamb chops.

I looked at the women who were left behind and couldn't help wondering whether they were feeling uncomfortable being in the open dressed as they were. Wouldn't it be normal to resent the lightly clad women on our side? Of course it would be, no question about it. And yet perhaps they feel they are pious, and will be rewarded in the afterlife, as our group would not. Was it so?

As I was having these thoughts, I saw one of the young women go over and stand facing the rock wall behind the slab on which they sat. She then proceeded to write on it with a piece of charcoal left by a previous picnicker, 'God leads astray whomsoever He will, and He guides whomsoever He will.'

As soon as Saba, our husky historian, saw what the young woman was doing he stopped eating, stood up and, turning to her, cried out across the water, 'What do you think you're doing? You're defacing the rock. This rock doesn't belong to you. Stop what you're doing immediately.'

She stopped at once and returned to her group. The older woman said something to her that we could not hear and she sat down again.

As I waited to see what was going to happen when the men returned I thought of a conversation I had recently had with a young man at Silwadi's, the juice shop in the centre of Ramallah.

I had noticed that he offered dates along with the citrus and other fruits he was juicing. I asked him how he used the dates. 'With milk,' he answered. 'It's a good mixture. After all, dates were the preferred food of the Prophet, peace be upon him.'

I then spoke to his assistant, the intense, silent one with a neat beard and large, drooping eyes that were downcast yet watchful and alert. I had often wondered about him.

He had once asked for my help in obtaining a permit for his sister-in-law, who was not being allowed to visit her husband in an Israeli jail. He thought I could help through the human rights organisation Al Haq, with which I'm associated. I didn't think Al Haq could help with this, but I did refer him to other organisations that I thought could. Today I asked him about the outcome. He told me that his sister-in-law now has a permit to visit but only once every six months. When she visits they stamp the permit and allow no other visit for another six months. He said they didn't want to stir the pot until after she visits.

'How long has this been going on?' I asked.

'Five years.'

'And how long is he in for?'

'He has eight life sentences.'

'Wow,' I exclaimed.

Immediately I regretted it. I knew I shouldn't have reacted in this manner. I should have praised his commitment or invoked God's blessing or implored Him to grant his family the ability to endure. Mine was definitely the wrong reaction. The man looked away, shutting me out and concentrating on his juicer.

In his essay 'The Last Temptation of Ivan Karamazov' Ariel Dorfman, the Argentine–Chilean novelist, playwright and essayist who wrote the famous play *Death and the Maiden*, states that torture 'presupposes … the abrogation of our capacity to imagine someone else's suffering, to dehumanise him or her so much that their pain is not our pain. It demands this of the torturer … but also demands of everyone else the same distancing, the same numbness, those who know and close their eyes, those who do not want to know and close their eyes, those who close their eyes and ears and hearts.'

The bearded men now returned from their foraging, carrying bundles of twigs and some logs for burning. The girls must have immediately complained about what had just happened and explained how Saba had stopped them from writing on the rock. The men commanded them to go back and cover every rock with holy graffiti large enough for all to see. They began to scrawl 'Allah, Allah' on every rock on their side.

This infuriated Saba. 'You want to show that you are more pious than we are, is that it?' he shouted across the water. 'Let me tell you that the Qur'an teaches, do not use the name of God in vain, do not write it where you cannot protect it. You're behaving in this way because you know we are Arabs, but when you face Israelis at a checkpoint you stand before them with bowed heads.'

'You don't know what you're talking about. You'd better not make stupid assumptions,' one of the men responded, ordering the girl to go on scrawling on the rock.

Saba began to move towards the water, wanting to cross to their side and confront them face-to-face. He was screaming now, 'This rock does not belong to you. You have no right to ruin it. It belongs to all of us. You have no right, no right whatsoever, to write on it. Do you hear me? No right.'

We were concerned that our hike would end up in a brawl, so we went after him and held him back.

After Saba calmed down, one of the bearded men guarding the rock on the opposite side spoke slowly and quietly: 'Have you now finished? Should I applaud you? Very well. But let me assure you, you know nothing. You don't know my contribution to the struggle, nor what I've done for the cause or how I behave towards the Jews.' Then he added, 'Don't think you can hide behind these foreigners you have brought with you. Just look at the clothes they're wearing. They're produced by those who exploit us and repress our people.'

Hearing this, I thought how appropriate that the screaming match should come down to the issue of clothing. Certainly our side was more colourfully dressed, with both men and women in jeans and red, yellow or orange T-shirts, while those on the other side wore depressing grey and black clothes as though they were in mourning.

I much preferred how our side looked and could not think that in wearing these colours we were contributing to the western domination of our region by supporting global capitalism any more than those on the rock on the other side of the water were doing.

I thought of the different worlds Palestinians now inhabit. One group is devoutly Islamic, while another is demonstratively secular, liberal and ever more concerned about being dominated and not allowed to get on with its way of life. The minority of remnant Christians assertively wear ever larger crosses around their necks or pinned to their lapels to counter the increasing numbers of more observant Muslims, both groups thus inadvertently sharing the same sort of religious extremism. It felt as though the small bit of Palestine left to us was being pulled apart by the opposing sides, with Israel situated in the middle, itself equally torn. This was all so unlike the tolerant Palestinian society of my younger years.

When I consider that to arrive at the site of the picnic we had to sneak in like thieves, rather than feeling that the place was ours to enjoy; that we had to suffer going through the numerous checkpoints in order to make it, and put up with being humiliated by the arrogant and chau-vinistic behaviour of Israeli soldiers … how can we not be on our guard, and not resort to self-righteousness, to holier-than-thou attitudes, to making claims of superiority and picking fights with each other?

We managed to calm Saba and an uneasy, temporary peace was made between the two sides, with neither coming any closer to a better understanding of the other though we could now proceed with our day. We all sat in a silence so deep that we could once again hear the water cascading down with great force from the Fawwar Spring and collecting in the pool that stretched between us as we continued with our picnics on our respective rocks, each soon becoming oblivious of the other. Then, after we had eaten and as we stretched our bodies, so differently clad, over the rocks in the sun, we listened to the water gurgling down the wadi on its way to the ancient city of Jericho.

18 DECEMBER

Today I had to go to the Jacir Palace hotel in Bethlehem for a meeting of the Independent Commission for Human Rights. The building, which had been turned into an Intercontinental Hotel in the late 1990s and opened for business just before the Second Intifada began, had once served as a boarding school where my aunt Mary was sent after her mother died during the First World War. I was not confident that I could manage to get there on my own after all the changes in the roads Israel has introduced. So I asked Hani Belbasi to drive me.

Hani was born in 1970, three years after the beginning of the Israeli occupation, and is blessed with a considerable measure of patience and resilience, both of which he needs to be able to survive as a driver during these sad times, when the road systems change constantly and are often blocked or made perilous. These qualities of his so impressed one of the soldiers at a checkpoint that Hani had passed through a number of times on the same day, each time being stopped and searched, that the soldier asked him, 'Don't you ever get fed up?' Hani answered him with a smile, saying, 'If I stopped coming you would have no one to search. You'd be out of work.'

Through his hard work, Hani's father managed to build a house with three apartments for himself and his children in the village of Kufr Aqab. Until a few years ago this suburb was within the borders of the Jerusalem municipality.

'It was nice when we were living all together,' Hani told me as he drove. 'Now we are split up. We had to move to a flat in Bab El Amoud, otherwise we would lose our Jerusalem residency. One day Israeli officials came and put an "X" on the wall of our Kufr Aqab house and this was the new border. Our house became outside Jerusalem. When we built it we were inside and took a mortgage from an Israeli bank. I had to pay $150 to get a copy of an aerial map from the municipality to confirm whether our house was inside or outside Jerusalem. I couldn't find it on the map. But when I described where it was the man there told me it was outside. So now we live most of the week in Jerusalem and my father goes for one day a week to Kufr Aqab. My father likes it there. He goes out to the garden, potters around or sits in the sun. He doesn't like to be in the apartment in Jerusalem, confined all day between four walls. But he has to be there or else he'll lose his Jerusalem residency.'

To get to Bethlehem Hani used the Walajeh road, which took a full hour even though it was a Friday with little traffic and we were not stopped. Walajeh is a very attractive small town to the east of Beit Jala. The land around it is forested and terraced, with a number of springs. The residents live in fear of having all their houses demolished because there are plans to build a new settlement there.

As he drove, Hani updated me on the latest developments in the investigation of his brother's murder. I happened to be with him when he learned that the Israeli police had arrested the perpetrator. This was a few months earlier, when he was driving me and the author Robert Macfarlane to the Mar Saba Monastery in the Jerusalem wilderness. We had left Ramallah, driving east, and just as we arrived at the Jabaa checkpoint Hani received a call on his mobile phone. I heard him answer in Hebrew and could see that he was disturbed.

'What is it?' I asked him when he finished. 'Is something wrong?'

In his quiet manner, he told me that it was a reporter from the Israeli daily *Yedioth Ahronoth*. 'He asked me to come for an interview and to bring with me a photograph of my brother.' I waited to hear more. Hani paused, then continued: 'Eleven years ago my brother was killed. This reporter has just told me they've found the man who murdered him.'

I had known Hani for a number of years but had never had any inkling of what he'd been through. I noted that in describing what happened he used the word 'killed' not 'martyred'. He told me how it happened.

'My brother was in the Malha district of Jerusalem when the passenger he was driving killed him with one bullet to his head. It went right through and was stopped by the car's side mirror, killing him at once. The engine continued running and the murderer was never found. This reporter tells me that the police have arrested him and the fact will be made public this evening, when it is announced on the six o'clock TV news.'

Now Hani told me that the Sunday after he left us he had met the journalist from *Yedioth*. After he handed over the photograph of his dead brother the journalist asked him what the family were going to do. Hani said that they had been advised to appoint a legal representative and had decided on an Arab lawyer. The journalist advised him to appoint an Israeli lawyer instead, claiming that the Palestinian Authority and Israel have decided not to take cases against each other and so an Arab lawyer could not handle the case. This is patently false. The journalist further argued that an Israeli lawyer will take a case against the state if need be and queried whether an Arab would be able to do this.

So Hani met with the lawyer from Tel Aviv who had been recommended to him and the lawyer named a fee of $15,000 for taking up a case against the accused to compensate the family, plus fifteen per cent of whatever he managed to get from the state as compensation to the parents for their loss. Hani agreed to these terms.

The police had meanwhile been trying to locate him and when he went to see them at the station he was told that they had suspected Yaakov (Jack) Teitel just a few weeks after the murder but 'did not have proof'. After the murder Hani and his family had been told nothing. Every day Hani had gone to ask, but the police were unhelpful and unpleasant, and finally told him, 'Don't come any more. We'll call you when we have something new.' He didn't hear from them again for the next eleven years. He and his family spent those eleven years in agony while the police 'knew' who the killer was but had not acted and revealed nothing.

'How do you and your family feel now?' I asked.

'My mother is distraught. It is as though the wound has been opened up once again. But on the other hand there is some solace. You know how people are. They were beginning to spread rumours that he was killed by Arabs for being an Israeli collaborator or for selling land.'

When Hani asked the police who was this man who had committed the murder, he was told, 'Well, he is like an Arab *mekhubal* [Hebrew for terrorist].'

'Why,' asked Hani, 'do you mean only Arabs are terrorists?'

Then the policeman corrected himself and admitted that this man was a terrorist – an unusual combination of being a non-Arab, a Jew and a terrorist.

The murdered brother had been twenty-two years old. His name was Sameer and he had been studying architectural engineering at Ort Technical School in West Jerusalem, the only son of the Belbasi family who was pursuing a college-level education and had the promise of becoming a professional. He was in his third year. He had finished his written end-of-year exams on 6 June at around 5 o'clock in the afternoon and had been seen by an older brother at Damascus Gate, waiting in his taxi for passengers. 'I haven't been able to work for the past ten days while preparing for my exams,' he had told his brother. 'Let me work for two hours, then I'll go home.'

That same afternoon Teitel, an American Jew on a visit to Israel, had hired a car at the Eldan Rental Agency and parked it near the Holy Land Hotel. He then went to the city centre in search of an Arab to kill. He found Sameer. Before leaving the United States he had taken apart a pistol, concealed the metal parts inside a video recorder and the plastic parts in his coat pocket. Once in Israel he purchased 200 rounds and practised shooting, all the while collecting intelligence. He told Sameer to drive him to the Holy Land Hotel, near where the Arab village of Malha once stood, now replaced by a huge Israeli shopping mall. As Hani passed the place during our drive, he pointed out exactly where his brother had been murdered. The hotel was up the hill. The road was deserted and ran through a forest. On the way the American talked about the weather to ensure from his accent that the driver was an Arab. Near the hotel, he asked him to stop the car, then fired a bullet into his head. The engine continued to run. The Jewish-American murderer left the car, retrieved his own, parked nearby and drove home.

That night Hani had come home exhausted after a hard day's work. He found his mother worried that it was already ten o'clock and Sameer had not returned, but she did not want to wake up her husband. Hani told her not to worry, said he would turn up soon and went to bed. One hour past midnight relatives called to say that the police were trying to contact them. Hani telephoned and the police asked him to come to the station. There he was told that something had happened and Sameer was dead. Hani asked to see him, but was told this was not possible as his body had been sent for an autopsy at the Abu Kbir Hospital.

When they went back and broke the news to their mother she collapsed and has never been well since. She became diabetic and her mind began to unravel. The father, who used to work on the Israeli side, could not continue. Ten days later the police returned the car, still with Sameer's blood splattered inside. It brought everything back. The mother cried, 'Here is my son's car, but where is he?' So much did the car remind them of Sameer that they could not keep it and decided to dispose of it as quickly as possible, even at a loss. They didn't even want to see it with a dealer on the East side, so they sent it over to a garage on the West and only got half its market value.

The day after the murder the police told them to go to Abu Kbir to retrieve the body. The father could not face this ordeal so Hani went, accompanied by three cars full of relatives. When he entered the refrigerated morgue with bodies all around he fainted and had to be revived. When Sameer's corpse was brought home he saw the hole in the side of the head through which the bullet had passed. They also noticed that the chest was stitched and someone thought the body had been hollowed and filled with cotton wool. They suspected that at Abu Kbir Sameer's organs had been stolen.

There certainly is a strong possibility that this is not mere paranoia: a few years after Sameer's death the director of the hospital was indicted for illegally selling human organs.

Hani's uncle urged that they bury the body without delay because of the June heat, and the presence of the corpse in the house was only making everyone miserable. They buried him that same evening and it was quickly over.

The next day the police summoned Hani. All day they interrogated him, demanding to know why he had killed his brother. The day after, at the wake, the police asked to have someone bring them over to the house because they were living near Ramallah, where the Israeli police did not feel safe going unescorted. Once at the house they questioned the neighbours, ostensibly to gather information to help them in the investigation but in effect sowing the seeds of suspicion that Hani's brother might have been killed by a fellow Arab. Then for eleven years they heard nothing more from the police.

After murdering Sameer, Teitel apparently returned home to the US, only to reappear in Israel a few years later as an immigrant living in the West Bank settlement of Eli. He then left again, returning after a short absence, this time with his Orthodox father, a dentist, and settling in Shuvot Rahel, near the West Bank settlement of Eli. By now he had learned from the Internet how to prepare bombs. He had also decided to kill and maim not only Arabs but also Jews who were opposed to settlers or those with whose ideas he simply did not agree. He discovered, again from a website, that the Messianic Jewish family of Ortiz was proselytising,* and he began collecting information about them. He contacted them under a false name from an Internet café, saying that he wanted to pray with the community. The deadliest bomb was sent to them. It was during the Jewish feast of Purim. He placed a box of chocolates at the door which was picked up by the son. When he opened it the bomb exploded, causing him serious injuries, but he survived. Yossi, the journalist who had contacted Hani, wanted him and his father to come to Tel Aviv to meet this victim's father. I suppose this was for a photo opportunity of an Arab and Jewish family victimised by a Jewish terrorist. But then the Jewish father said that his son was ill and he could not leave, asking if they would come to him at the settlement instead. Hani, being an agreeable sort, said, 'Why not?'

During the visit Hani learned that this family, which had received many threats, had installed cameras and captured Teitel on film. The father had taken the film to the police, but they did nothing. Then one day the father spotted Teitel at a supermarket and called the police, but still they did not

---

* Messianic Judaism blends evangelical Christian theology with elements of Jewish terminology and ritual. Its adherents believe that Jesus is not merely a man but the Jewish Messiah and 'God the Son' (one person of the Trinity) and that salvation is only achieved through acceptance of Jesus as one's saviour.

arrest him. The police did try to plant a security agent to work with him, but Teitel refused, insisting that he only worked alone.

Hani also learned that one month after killing Sameer in June 1997, Teitel had murdered a Palestinian shepherd, Isa Jabbarin. He had bought a gift for his former employer in the settlement of Sussia in the Hebron hills and rented a white Fiat. When he saw the shepherd, he stopped and asked him for directions to Jerusalem. Jabbarin leaned towards the car window, not understanding the question. Teitel pulled out his pistol and shot him twice in the head, killing him instantly. He then continued to the house of his former employer, ten minutes away from the murder scene, and presented them with the gift. He was arrested several days later in one of the area settlements because he was driving a car similar to the one he was driving when he killed the shepherd. He was questioned but once again he was released and returned to the US.

Hani's account of the Ortiz family is that although they are settlers themselves they claim to hate the other settlers and continue to live in the settlement only because they have no other home. They say they like the Arabs, and the father continues to fetch them from the villages and finds work for them at the settlement. 'See, an Arab painted my house,' he told Hani.

Ortiz also told the journalist that he had been getting death threats and never opened the door of his house without first checking. One time someone rang the bell and he opened the door just a slit, but as he did so a man took his picture and, along with those of ten other Messianic Jews with similar beliefs, it was printed on a poster with the caption that these Jews must be killed. Still the police did nothing.

But then Teitel began targeting more establishment Jews. Professor Zeev Sternhell, the Israeli historian who teaches at the Hebrew University in Jerusalem and who was writing articles critical of the settlers, now became a target. Teitel went to his house and placed a parcel bomb there with the intention of not killing but rather of maiming the professor, 'so that his face would show how ugly is his soul'.

Now the police were keeping watch and gathering evidence against Teitel until they had enough to capture him.

'Of course he pleaded insanity,' Hani told me. 'This is what is always said of Israeli Jews who murder Arabs. Mad and therefore not guilty. But as Professor Sternhell asked in court, how could someone insane be capable of smuggling weapons to Israel despite all the security measures and intentionally maim other Jews whose politics he does not like?'

When he asked his lawyer what punishment this Teitel was expected to receive, Hani was told he would probably be in prison for some twelve years. With the various pardons he would be given, it was unlikely in the present circumstances in Israel that he would spend that long behind bars.

Hani could not be aware of how hearing this was opening up old wounds for me from the time when the Israeli police so callously and cruelly withheld information about my own father's assassin and how, as in Hani's case, they tried to deflect us from the real murderer. As we later learned, the police knew all along who was responsible, but of all the various suspects the one who was the murderer was never interrogated or brought to justice. They just let him go free, torturing us for many, many years with the uncertainty and pain of not knowing the truth about his identity. How can I ever forgive them?

4 JANUARY 2010

My wife, Penny, and I went today to Bethlehem to look at the work of Banksy, the British street artist, on the Annexation Wall there. This conflict and the methods Israel uses to repress Palestinians are producing responses in many parts of the world. Banksy is one artist – but not the only one – who has come to express his feelings about the situation using the wall as his canvas.

We took the Walajeh road heading south-west on a circular route to Bethlehem, which is directly south of Jerusalem, in order to avoid the checkpoint between the two cities. Once Hani had shown me the way I could drive by myself. We were stopped at the Walajeh checkpoint, which I had heard also checks whether those crossing it have paid their taxes to Israel, just to make life more complicated. But there was no big delay. The road meandered through beautiful hills overlooking forested valleys with ancient villages spread all around. One of these, Battir, which lies further east, is famous for its aubergines and has some of the earliest examples of terraced agriculture. The planned route of the Annexation Wall will destroy these fields that have been cultivated for many centuries. So extensive would be the loss that in a rare case of coordinated action Israelis and Palestinians are working together to prevent the wall from being built there. Close by stood the village of New Walajeh, which was built following the Nakba – the Palestinian Catastrophe – of 1948 by the inhabitants of the original village on the hill opposite after they were forced out. Now the Israeli authorities are claiming the houses were built without a permit and have issued demolition orders. If they carry out their threats very few houses would remain and the nearby settlement will spread and swallow

With no access to the nearby Mediterranean, many drawings by West Bank children feature seaside images.

the village land, completing the isolation of Jerusalem on the south-eastern side from the nearby Palestinian towns and villages.

As we drove along the narrow winding road and listened to music, Penny and I reviewed the last decade. We found it full of wars. We counted five that had taken place in our immediate region (which does not include Afghanistan), each more brutal than the last. The Second Intifada was the first, followed by the Israeli invasion of West Bank cities, then the Iraq war, the second Lebanon war and the war on the Gaza Strip. In the beginning I had refused to acknowledge the Intifada that was raging around me and concentrated instead on my writing. I now realize that this established a pattern for me. With every war a new book. Five wars, five books.

From the top of the hill we looked down at the violated valley and saw a beautiful band of blue haze. The sun was illuminating the mist formed by the moisture-laden air that had settled in the valley. It was not like the ordinary haze that can sometimes be seen veiling our hills. It had density, substance and the opaqueness of the purest pervasive blue, like a shroud that had descended from the heavens into the valley and spread along its entire length, linking the two sides, Arab and Jewish, so often divided by walls of steel and concrete but also of hatred and lies.

Up the hill we found the so-called DCO [District Coordination Office] checkpoint abandoned and drove through. There is no wall here.

From the heights of Beit Jala, where we entered, we could see the road to the Gush Etzion settlement 'bloc' around Hebron, with the tunnel piercing the hill on which we stood. The ancient city of Beit Jala, attractive and tidy with many of its old buildings preserved, has been violently penetrated. Fortunately, it has not been spoiled by high-rise blocks, as happened in Ramallah. We crossed the town, drove into Bethlehem and joined the main road that used to connect the city of Christ's nativity with Jerusalem. Had it not been for the checkpoint, this would have been the road we took to Jerusalem.

As we approached the wall that bisects the road we saw the first of Banksy's works, a young girl frisking an Israeli soldier, his gun laid on the side. Effective, I thought. Then we came upon one with a dotted line and scissors, as though the wall were made of cardboard and was doomed eventually to be cut through. Next, to one side, was a mouse with a slingshot, painted on a small concrete slab that used to be part of a barrier but was now abandoned at the edge of the road. We parked the car and walked along the wall. I tried hard to figure out its course and what lies on the other side, but this was not easy because of the twists and turns.

No longer the thriving city I used to know, Bethlehem was now a punished city cut off from East Jerusalem and the rest of the West Bank, its lifeline, and thrown to the dogs. There was the sense that the inhabitants had been chased out and banished, the gate closed behind them and the key thrown in the gutter.

We saw taxis waiting on the Bethlehem side, where the wall divides the highway that once used to be such a busy road. They were desperate for work and were disappointed that we didn't need a car. To their right were two long pedestrian passageways bordered by metal grilles, one for entering and the other for exiting Jerusalem. In the morning they would be busy with those Palestinians fortunate enough to have permits to work in Israel. There was no one using them now. As I walked away I recalled a documentary I had seen about this checkpoint that featured an Israeli violinist who would come every morning at daybreak, take his old violin out of its case and play it to cheer the labourers, penned in and herded like cattle, as they waited to be allowed into Israel to earn their meagre livings. It was not clear what the workers made of this old man as their sleepy eyes stared blankly through the grille. He never spoke; he just played his instrument with a pained expression on his face.

We walked along the wall, which was covered with graffiti expressing horror, the transience of this monstrosity and rage against the Israelis for putting it up. In one of the wall's loops we met a woman with tightly combed-back hair and a purposeful, intelligent look. She was walking away from her house, taking the mandatory detour to town. I asked her what was behind this part of the wall, hazarding a guess that Rachel's Tomb would be there.

'No, it's not,' she said. 'That is the car park.'

So they made the loop around only to provide space for a car park for Jewish worshippers.

'This is our house over there,' she then told me. It was in a bay surrounded on three sides by the wall. 'We had four shops by the road which are now closed.'

'Did you consider suing?' I asked.

'We did, but they would not listen to us. We appointed a lawyer, but there was no way. No one cares for us. We lost our business. Our children are not developing normally. Imagine waking every day to see the wall before you. They have lost their happy childhood. Their growth is stunted. But no one cares, no one thinks of us. This is how it is. Our lives are destroyed.'

I walked towards her house. She had a 'Merry Christmas' sign and a wreath over the door, lonely greetings that no passer-by would read or see. Their house had always stood on the busy main street, where tourists would stop and buy from the shops below their flat. Now, like the rest of the city, it was banished, isolated, penalised, tucked away in a small enclosure surrounded on three sides by an immense concrete wall, alone and desolate. But who was responsible for planning the course of the wall, I wondered? Surely it must have been tremendously more costly to make the wall loop in this fashion rather than run in a straight line. Surely the cement manufacturers, steel importers, construction companies vying for lucrative contracts and those eager to lay their hands on Palestinian land sequestered on the Israeli side must have exerted their influence. No wonder Israelis are not allowed to visit this side of the wall. How ashamed they would be if they saw what was being done to their neighbours in their name. There can be no justification, on security or any other pretext, for such a wall.

The real reason for this wall is to sever Bethlehem from Jerusalem. Israel is remapping the whole area, extending into the heart of the West Bank so as to encircle East Jerusalem with a thick chain of Jewish settlements and isolate the city from the Arab towns of Bethlehem to the south and Ramallah to the north. This is quite clear to me.

In an empty clearing created by the wall north of where the woman's house stood an artist had placed an installation in the form of a catapult. We went up to look at it and two boys no older than thirteen joined us. They were taking a cigarette break from their work of selling postcards to the non-existent tourists. 'We are in the tourist business,' they told us when we enquired what they did. They had obviously come here to smoke without being detected. Before the wall was built this was prime land that could be seen from the highway; now it is an enclosed area where youngsters come for a smoke out of sight of their elders.

What desolation has been wrought on the entrance to this ancient city!

We left this dismal scene and continued our tour of the wall. Next to the house was the message 'I want my ball back' and below it, 'Thank you'. If the children who live here should lose their ball behind the wall they would have no way of retrieving it.

When we emerged from this miserable labyrinth of concrete we were accosted by a desperate man selling rosaries who pestered me to buy from him. Other shopkeepers met us with the complaint, 'Where are the tourists you brought?' Like everywhere else, those in the tourist business cannot help seeing every visitor as a potential purchaser and nothing else. It was all most trying.

From the restaurant where we had lunch we could see the flourishing summit of Jabal Abu Gniem, which Israelis call Har Homa. Already developed, this is another piece of the Israeli construction plan to encircle East Jerusalem with more Jewish settlements.

A film-maker had taught residents of the Aida refugee camp in Bethlehem video-mapping techniques and had asked them to represent various aspects of camp life showing how their space and their surroundings had changed over time. One of the subjects was a mother whose daughter had a hereditary disease that required weekly infusions at the Palestinian Al-Maqased Hospital in East Jerusalem. She mapped out the various routes she and her sick daughter had to take to get to the hospital and how much more complicated the wall had made their journey. As the lines projected on to the screen became increasingly entangled and we saw how complicated the Israelis had rendered our lives, I became more and more convinced that we were living next to a mad people.

20 JANUARY

I am just back from a day spent in Jerusalem. It is not the city I used to know and enjoy. When Father was alive he was optimistic, believing that there was a possibility of compromise and a shared Jerusalem. I don't know where he found his optimism. Anyway, the Israeli leadership soon snuffed it out entirely, from greed and the arrogance of power.

In his lifetime my father presented me with a different kind of challenge. He was a proponent of peaceful coexistence and it seemed he could see no evil. He so much wanted things to work out, and to see a Palestinian state established alongside Israel. Every weekend in the summer we would drive to the sea near Jaffa. (It strikes me that the Jewish settlements are intended to sever Palestinian population centres in the West Bank not only from each other but also from those Arab communities in Israel.) From 1967 to 1991 the borders between Israel and the Occupied Territories were removed and everyone could travel freely between the two areas. Marriages took place between Arab couples across the divide. Now I walk in the main shopping street of East Jerusalem, Salah ed-Din, and notice that the wire fence surrounding the Israeli Ministry of Justice is higher than it used to be. The ministry is housed in a building captured from the Jordanian authorities and situated in the occupied part of the city. It serves as a reminder to those working within it that they should constantly contrive legal excuses for the perpetuation of the occupation or else risk losing everything, including the offices where they work. Across the street is the District Court, where I used to go with my father when it served as an Arab court under Jordan. The Israeli government seized it and moved our own court to the building that used to be

Ramallah's vegetable market. That's how respectful they were of our need for a judiciary.

Standing before the courthouse I thought how different my father's experience was from mine. Many of the Israeli Jews he knew were those whom he had met during the British Mandate period. Having that talent for seeing and bringing out the best in people, he continued to believe that it would be possible to live together. He introduced me to many of his old acquaintances and I could see the respect they had for him. Among them was the Iraqi Jew at the Land Survey Department who had extensive knowledge of classical Arabic literature and regaled us with his recitations of Arabic poetry every time we visited his office. But then those old-timers who felt an affinity with the Arabs among whom they had lived in peace for many years were replaced by the angry ones. The worst of these was the so-called Custodian of Absentee Property. He was also an Iraqi Jew, who claimed to belong to a rich family in Baghdad that had lost all its property when they immigrated to Israel. He was therefore happy to be in a position that enabled him to punish Palestinian Arabs by keeping their property in the hands of the Israeli state. My father handled a number of cases where, despite the stringent Absentee Property Law, he was able to find loopholes that enabled some properties to be restored. But Shukarji would not have it. I remember him well. He had a round, bloated face and a large belly. He was short and when seated he looked like an inflated ball behind a desk covered with papers and files. He never smiled and his favourite word was 'no', which was his answer to all our requests, accentuated by a definitive shaking of his bulbous head.

Yet my father never gave up. Soon he would return with another line of argument to put before this impossible petty official. That is how formidable he was.

But the new Israelis have become so much worse since the time I worked with him. I used to think that once the old generation of Israeli leaders went, most of whom came from Poland, like Ben-Gurion, Begin and Peres, the younger ones born here would understand better and be more likely to make peace. But the new generation of leaders is even more hawkish. I failed to realize that it is the colonial system that produces these personalities, with their tactics and racist positions, and that this system was not weakening with time.

As I drive in the transformed city I find myself asking: could Father not see? He took things so personally and felt the Arab defeat very deeply, as though he himself were responsible for it. Why did he have to keep on trying in his professional and political work to achieve the impossible?

I see it now: a highway running through the property that belonged to the soft-spoken Turjuman, my father's client. Highway 1 was planned many years ago to divide the western side of the city from the eastern and render the Arab side a ghetto with limits to its potential for expansion. Roads are more effective barriers than walls, as Israeli planners know all too well. Not a single Arab has been allowed to build in what used to be the seam zone, the no-man's-land between East and West Jerusalem. Land owned by Arabs was confiscated and given to Jewish developers, who built fancy hotels on it. All this was planned a long time ago and was being finalised while you, Father, persisted in your futile struggle to invoke the laws of justice and reasonableness. You would say to Shukarji, 'But Turjuman, my client lost almost everything in 1948 and now you want to take from him the little he has left.' Yes, Father, that is precisely what they wanted to do. They are merciless. Why could you not accept it and see the evil they are capable of? Why did you not direct your energies elsewhere?

Clearly you couldn't. You had to take the impossibly difficult cases and endure the full consequences of frustration and failure, refusing to accept the facts, the sinister policy that was driving the Israeli authorities you were determined to confront. You gave up your life to hopeless causes and left mother a widow and your children orphaned.

We would be returning home from Jerusalem and my father would ask me, 'Are you hungry?'

'Starving. How about you?'

'These days I don't get hungry. It is not the way it was. Life for me has lost its flavour.'

I could sense that my father was depressed and not too communicative. Yet on one occasion we managed a rare intimate conversation when I confided that I was finding it very difficult to adjust to the broken-down court system.

'How will I manage under these conditions?' I asked him.

'You will,' he assured me. 'You'll find your own individual way. I am certain of it.'

Yes, Father. You were right. I have found my way, though it took many, many years.

4 APRIL

For over a hundred years with a few significant breaks, every year on the Saturday before Orthodox Easter Sunday, the Main Street in Ramallah is transformed with numerous groups of scouts parading and playing music. The pavements are lined with tens of thousands of onlookers from within and outside the city.

It is not much of a parade. The trumpeters mostly play out of tune and the drumming, though enthusiastic, is far too noisy and often off tempo. Yet throughout my life I have tried never to miss *Sabt el Nur*, the Procession of the Light, when the light 'miraculously' emerges from Christ's tomb in the Church of the Holy Sepulchre, where the Greek Patriarch awaits. He then emerges from the small, dark chamber and proceeds to assure the throngs gathered at the church from all over the world that the miracle of the light has happened yet again. The flame is then transported to the various Christian towns throughout Palestine to light their churches before the celebration of Easter Sunday. Some take it to their homes and attempt to keep it flickering throughout the year. For me, annual occasions like this one constitute important markers of time and display the changing circumstances that this troubled town of ours has been through.

For the small minority of Palestinian Christians, most of whom are Greek Orthodox, Easter is the most important holy feast. It is at the time of year when the weather in Palestine is at its best. It is also the most colourful feast. It used to be accompanied by a number of other festivals, such as the Feast of Annunciation, known as *Sitna Mariam*, when Christians and Muslims camped out for three days on the hill outside the Old City of Jerusalem's Lion's Gate. But since the Israeli occupation of Jerusalem this festival has been cancelled. Other ceremonies, such as the Way of the Cross along the Via Dolorosa in the Old City, continue to be celebrated, but mainly by tourists from around the world, not by Palestinian Christians from outside Jerusalem, who are restricted from entering the Holy City. So what remains is *Sabt el Nur*, which has been celebrated in Jerusalem for the past 1,200 years.

According to Naseeb Shaheen in *A Pictorial History of Ramallah*, before the Nakba, which divided Palestine, young men from Ramallah and other Palestinian towns went to Jerusalem to obtain the light. He writes that while mostly the young men from Ramallah won, often 'serious' disputes 'broke out over who would be first to obtain the light'. The most serious disagreements were often between the young men from Ramallah and Lydda.

For the past twenty-two years it has not been possible for Ramallah people to get the flame from Jerusalem themselves, so there has not been much of a chance to compete over who gets it first. Now they have to wait at the Kalandia checkpoint, which separates the two cities, for the flame to be delivered.

On arrival it is taken to the town's main square, the Manarah (literally 'lighthouse'), where it is awaited by the Greek Orthodox priest along with other officials and dignitaries. They have arrived at the square at the head of some eight groups of Scouts from Ramallah and adjoining Christian towns, Jifna, Aboud, Birzeit and Taybeh, as well as from the nearby refugee camps. They also include Scouts from the Islamic Club of Ramallah. Despite its essential Christian significance this celebration brings together Christians and Muslims. And on this occasion a Scout group from the mixed Israeli town of Lydda in Israel also took part in the parade.

This year Penny and I did not have to join the crowds standing on the pavements. We were invited to watch the procession from a friend's balcony, the director of the Mattin Group, a policy and law research company whose office overlooks Main Street. As I climbed the stairs I remembered how this office had been destroyed by the Israeli army during the 2002 Israeli invasion of Ramallah, which happened at around this time of the year. That was one of the few years when there was no *Sabt el Nur* celebration, just as there were none during the first few years following the 1967 war, when the Israeli occupation began, nor the first two years of the First Intifada in 1988 and 1989. How often I had yearned for the time when we Palestinians could celebrate our feast in peace, in an independent Palestine free from the harassments of the soldiers of a foreign army in control of our life. This has yet to happen, though it is now possible for the Scouts to pin the Palestinian flag on their uniforms and have the flag-bearer walk in the lead. Flags are hoisted in abundance in Palestinian cities and villages and yet these Scouts parading in the street today are unable to camp out in the countryside because most of it is still under foreign control.

I will never forget an incident that took place in 1990, the first time after the start of the Intifada that the Israeli army allowed the procession to take place. They had stip-ulated that no Palestinian flag could be flown. But some enthusiastic young man had climbed to the roof of the Salah Pharmacy overlooking the Manarah and placed a flag there. It was spotted by some of the organisers responsible for securing the permit. They immediately asked a young man to climb up and remove it. He did so, as we watched with bated breath to see whether some Israeli sniper would shoot him before he could get it down. When he got to the flag, he proceeded to wrap it up so carefully and lovingly, and before putting it away he brought it up to his lips and kissed it. Then he tucked it away in his shirt and came down. We all watched spellbound. I wondered where this young person – who must have been born after the Israeli occupa-tion, since when flying the flag has always been an offence – learned how he must treat the flag.

The first group of Scouts passing by beat at their drums with amazing assertiveness and enthusiasm, as others blew into their trumpets making terrible sounds. To my surprise the next group (and this was an innovation this year) played bagpipes. As this is not an instrument that is played in Palestine, I wondered who could have taught them to play it. From the time when it had British officers, the Jordanian army has been adept at playing the instrument; could they have been taught in Jordan or by soldiers from the Jordanian army? The other innovation was the wearing of capes, some white and some red, with crosses prominent on their uniform, making them look like young crusaders.

The Palestinian police handled the situation superbly. All the traffic was diverted, there was order and not a single fight broke out despite the large numbers of people milling around. Everyone seemed to be having a good time on this warm spring day.

The flame was duly delivered and on the return journey from the Manarah to the Greek Orthodox Church in the Old City of Ramallah, I noticed that the priest had given the flame that was to be carried to the Muslim Prime Minister of the Palestinian Authority, walking by his side, and another to the Muslim District Governor, walking on the other side. Looking down from our balcony at this example of religious harmony brought out a wistful yearning for that time in Palestine when this ceremony began to be celebrated in Ramallah. It was so normal then for Christians, Jews and Muslims of this land to participate in each other's religious feasts and celebrate together and feel enhanced rather than threatened by the presence of the other monotheistic religions that lived peacefully together for hundreds of years.

Occupation Diaries

17 MAY

All day today and yesterday (as I was going over the second proofs of my book *A Rift in Time*) the thought that kept running through my mind was that the veneer of civilisation and decency in Israel is getting thinner. But I was wrong, it has vanished entirely. We were waiting for Noam Chomsky to arrive later in the afternoon from Amman. Rita Giacaman, who established and for many years headed the Institute of Community and Public Health at Birzeit University, and her husband, Mustafa Barghouti, who heads Al Mubadara, the Palestinian National Initiative, had invited us to a dinner in his honour. And on Tuesday we were hosting a dinner for him at our house. Tomorrow, Monday, he was to give a public lecture in Birzeit University. Then the phone rang and we learned from Rita that the Israelis would not allow him entry. An order from the Ministry of the Interior prohibited him from entering via the Allenby Bridge because they don't like his ideas and don't like the fact that he is speaking at Birzeit. Even though I had somehow expected it, I still felt fear when it happened – fear at what Israeli excesses might come to, and fear at what would become of us. This day of waiting reminded me of earlier times, with the difference that we were all so much older and more seasoned.

Even without the pleasure of Chomsky's company we did join Rita and Mustafa for dinner. Gracious Rita refused to cancel. Mustafa spent most of the evening answering calls on his mobile. He spoke to a great many news agencies from around the world. His line was that if Israel would not allow someone like Chomsky to enter the country, was it any surprise what they did to us?

As it turned out, by refusing entry to a world-famous

32

intellectual like Chomsky, who is not exactly a wanted terrorist, the Israeli authorities have done themselves a lot of harm.

18 MAY

To Birzeit University to hear Chomsky on video link from Amman. In his quiet, intelligent and thorough manner, he went through the US position in the world and the relationship between the US and Israel, reminding us of the basis of this relationship and the changes that it has gone through over time. The important thing is not to believe that it will end any time soon. Mother's hope that she would see the end before she died was folly, and it is unlikely that I will see it either. The important thing is not to give up.

I was very happy to hear Chomsky confirm my position on the desirable and feasible future. The two-state solution is the only realistic one. It is just a step, one that will lead to new relationships in the area. But ultimately the model to follow is that of the Ottoman period, when the whole of the Great Rift Valley east of the Mediterranean was one unified region. Not that we should call for the return of anything resembling Ottoman rule – the Ottomans were brutal and inefficient – but rather a return to the way things were organised then, with communities and cultures united. Using the relationships that existed between the ethnic groups in the region prior to division into nation states is not a bad model to consider.

5 JUNE

Sometimes it takes a long time for the significance of events to be understood. Now, over a year after the Gaza war (and forty-three years to the day after the 1967 war that brought the Israeli occupation upon us), I can see how this time Israel has gone too far. It might also have lost whatever intimidating deterrent value its threat of waging a similar war against the Palestinians might have had. Ten years ago, Israeli citizens were not forbidden by law from entering Palestinian cities in the West Bank, nor was the Gaza Strip under siege as it is now. It is much easier to impose your view of the people living behind the ghetto walls when you don't allow your citizens to encounter them personally and see for themselves. If we go back to Palestine seventy years ago, we find a number of mixed Jewish and Arab communities, both cities and villages, which for centuries before the British Mandate were able to coexist. And if we go back further still, we find that the entire eastern Mediterranean under the Ottoman Empire was without borders demarcating what became the Arab nation states of Syria, Jordan and Lebanon, and later the Jewish state of Israel.

The present is a very different story.

'We aren't North America or Western Europe,' Ehud Barak, Israel's Defence Minister, told the commandos who participated in the deadly raid on the Gaza-bound Freedom Flotilla last Monday. 'We live in the Middle East, in a place where there is no mercy for the weak and there aren't second chances for those who don't defend themselves.'

This very same Barak is fond of describing Israel as 'a villa in the jungle'. Israeli politicians like him appear congenitally incapable of conceiving of any other way of life for their country than that of a fortress state with a strong army, living by the gun in an area populated by millions of Arabs. Israel makes no effort to build bridges, communicate peacefully, learn the language or find a place

Gaza's isolation is also mine. Now thanks to Turkey and to internationals like the Swedish crime writer Henning Mankell, this has been broken.

for itself and integrate – except by force and the language of power and violence.

But just as Israel's present leaders are fond of distinguishing between the untamed Middle East jungle and their sparkling, untainted colonial white villa, so they indulge in their favourite fantasy: that their country is part of the West. Why should they have open borders that would allow in their 'terrorist neighbours'? Better keep the country sealed and segregated in apartheid-style splendid isolation, while retaining their links to the West by air and sea.

The events of 31 May 2010 on the high seas, when Israel attacked the flotilla, killing nine people and injuring scores of others on the Turkish boat the *Mavi Marmara*, upset this false equilibrium. Sailing aboard the ships that came to challenge the Israeli policy of keeping Gaza under siege were hundreds of Westerners, many of them renowned for their contributions to the best that the West has to offer: writers, politicians and advocates for human rights. Israeli propagandists should have thought twice before describing them as terrorists.

One of the justifications offered for attacking the boats was that they were challenging Israel's policy towards Gaza. But this was precisely the declared objective of the organisers. They were members of civil society who had despaired of their governments' accepting their responsibility to enforce international law and protect the human rights of a besieged population of 1.5 million people.

Israel either doesn't understand the power of mass movements or – arrogantly, hubristically – ignores it. This alone, and the reflexive use of force against anyone challenging its policies towards the Occupied Palestinian Territories, can explain why it struck so hard at the flotilla. It was the same reaction as the leaders of Israel had after the Palestinians' first uprising. 'Break their bones,' Prime Minister Rabin ordered his army, so that unarmed protesters would cower in fear and stay at home. The policy did not work then, nor would it this time round.

The siege of Gaza and the struggle to end it are significant enough. Even more significant is the fact that this time help came from Turkey. It has been almost a hundred years since the demise of the Ottoman Empire, whose four-century rule over the Arabs has gone down in history as our Dark Ages. It has taken all this time for the wounds to heal and now help for the Gazans has come from Turkey in the form of a Turkish boat manned by Turks who were willing to risk a lot to come to the aid of fellow Muslims. This is a most important transformation with more far-reaching repercussions than the immediate impact on the besieged Gazans.

Israel and Turkey began with a number of similarities. They are both the product of late-nineteenth-century nationalism and both to a large extent created a new language, opting to separate from the past. In the case of Turkey this was done by changing the alphabet and in the case of Israel by opting against the use of Yiddish. One consequence of this is the inability of most Israelis to read the vast literature in Yiddish, just as the Turks today cannot read any of their literature written prior to 1923.

Both states were also responsible for the expulsion of hundreds of thousands of people from the land where they established themselves: the Armenians from Turkey and parts of historic Armenia and the Palestinians from the part of Palestine that became Israel. In each case the modern state is unable and unwilling to come to terms with its past. Israel denies the Nakba, Turkey the Armenian expulsion.

In both countries the military enjoys special power and status: the armed forces have a central role in politics and the control of the state and its policies and direction.

Both of course are allies of the US.

Gaza's isolation is also mine. Now, thanks to Turkey and to internationals like the Swedish crime writer Henning Mankell, this has been broken. I met Henning last year when he participated in the Palestine Literary Festival and I took him on a walk in our hills. Today the *Guardian* newspaper published his diary. Immediately after reading it I sent him this email:

> Dear Henning
>
> I can't begin to describe how I felt when I read your diary in today's *Guardian*. It is as though after decades of suffering in silence (today marks the forty-third anniversary of the occupation), with both the cause of my suffering being denied and my experience of it called suspect, after years and years of hardship and pain, there was finally vindication.
>
> You write that your aim was [to show] that 'deeds, not words' are what are important and that 'only action can provide proof of your words'. Your actions followed by your words in the article published today have provided ample proof that you have acted on your conviction. You have not just helped the just cause of Palestine. You also saved me and many others around the world from the cynicism of the harsh world we live in. I was so profoundly moved when I read how your ship was carrying cement, reinforcement bars and prefabricated wooden houses for the people of Gaza. To realize how their suffering and homelessness have not gone unfelt by one so far in the north of the globe, in Sweden, and through you and your

colleagues, the rest of the world is more important than the strongest possible words of condemnation or solidarity.

And Israeli leaders don't tire of repeating how their country is 'a villa in a jungle'!

Warm greetings from Ramallah.

Raja

7 JUNE

This is how it will be with the Gaza flotilla: Israel commits an obvious violation, attacking the *Mavi Marmara* in international waters, killing and kidnapping people, and, in order not to have the truth revealed, confiscating all video-recording devices without authority, and illegally jamming all communications with the ship. They allow only evidence in their favour – highly doctored, of course – to emerge. Today they published an interview with the ship's captain in *Ha'aretz*, in which he is reported as saying that he tried to prevent the passengers from being violent. Now they want a commission of inquiry to be chaired by an Israeli high court judge. This is with the 'agreement' of the US, which has 'insisted' on what is of course an Israeli demand but sounds better coming from the US.

8 JUNE

I was feeling somewhat uplifted by the solidarity of people around the world with the inhabitants of Gaza. I raised the topic with an old lawyer who has been in legal practice since the British Mandate period.

I was enthusiastically babbling on about the *Mavi Marmara* when he said, 'It is all a lot of talk but no action, nothing will come of it. I will never forget Keith Rotch in the Mandate administration. The clerk at his office would bring him a report about a demonstration outside with pamphlets and banners. "Do they have guns?" he would ask. "Do they have a single bullet?" "None at all," the officer would answer. So he would take the report and mark it "PA". Do you know what this meant? Put aside. And so it would be put on the shelf to gather dust. Nothing more would happen. What will prevent Israel from going on with its policies? Words? Will those countries speaking out send an army to force Israel to do what they want? Of course not, so ... "PA".'

11 JUNE

Last night I saw the al-Jazeera International investigative report of the assault on the *Mavi Marmara*.

What a difference having al-Jazeera English has made. I no longer have to hear the biased reporting on CNN or BBC World, which only makes me more annoyed and despairing.

I hope I manage to purge myself of this deep anger before I travel in two months' time, otherwise I will be totally ineffective in speaking about my new book. It is easier to dismiss an angry spokesman.

Mustafa Barghouti was recently in the US, speaking to politicians at the White House. He pointed out that he and his supporters are practising exactly what the US has always called for, non-violent resistance, but Israel is responding with violence. He asked why the US doesn't hold back the Israelis. The answer was: 'The Palestinians must not get all the way to the Israeli side and the Palestinian police must block them from reaching the Israelis.' Mustafa replied, 'It is the Israelis who come to us. The demonstrations are against the wall that is built inside Palestinian territory. It is not we who come to them, they come to us.'

The politicians did not understand the point, or pretended not to.

16 JUNE

This morning I was working in the garden, weeding around the coriander patch, when I heard Penny shouting and calling for me to come inside. I rushed in. Penny was in the bathroom, standing by the floor drain and looking very rattled.

'What is it?' I asked.

'I was cleaning the drain and put my hand in and found a snake inside. I could feel its body in my hand.'

She was trembling in fright.

What would a snake be doing in our drain, I wondered?

I did not dare probe with my hand, so I brought a stick and poked around in the drain. I could feel something long, but it was hard. If it were a snake it would have moved away by now. Unless it is a fossilised one!

Upon further investigation, it turned out that the roots of the cherry tree, or the pomegranate, both of which were growing not far from the drain, must have found their way in as they searched for water in our dry soil. Perhaps I should have thought of this struggle for survival when I planted these two trees in such close proximity to each other. I suspected, though, that the greater villain must have been the cherry tree, because it had been showing signs of disease which I was told might be due to excessive ferti-lising, proof that it does not always pay to have stronger, more aggressive roots.

20 JUNE

Just after the Palestinian Authority took control of Ramallah in 1996 the new mayor appointed by Arafat decided to sandblast the storefronts and remove all graffiti from the buildings. This was a welcome facelift for the city with its façades besmirched by the excessive zeal of the various Palestinian factions. The problem was that the cleaning operations were carried out without taking any precautions. The fronts of the buildings being treated were not covered with protective sheeting. As a result clouds of dust polluted the air, making it difficult to breathe, and everything was covered in a film of grey powder. It seemed that the cleaning operation was being done to beautify the place for the benefit not of the residents but of others whom our new mayor was trying to impress. But who?

Today as I drove through the city I saw huge posters advertising bank loans, announcing USAID projects and promoting the new kind of life they claim is available and possible: 'There are no limits to what you can dream of,' they declare. Before, we had none of these billboards that now dominate our skies, inviting us to borrow, buy and dream, as long as we do not dream of travelling beyond the borders of our own small city without being stopped by the occupation army. Nor did we have the opportunity of obtaining credit before the false peace. Now the banks dominate our lives as their billboards dominate our skies. None of these banks were here before the Oslo Accords. Israel would not allow them. The only banks we had were branches of the three main Israeli banks, which offered very limited credit. They left when the Israeli army evacuated the main cities. As a result of the generous mortgages now on offer, building activity has increased significantly.

There is nothing inherently wrong with development and construction; it is rather the way the building is taking place that is objectionable. It seems to be happening in a frenzy of desperate hyperactivity. It is more important to get the construction underway with no regard to the effect it has on people's quality of life and health. Mounds of sand are dumped on pavements and spill into streets, despite these being public spaces. No attempt is made at containing them, so when the wind blows everything gets coated with layers of sand and cement. No scaffolding or protective cover is used during construction, so there is constant noise from the pneumatic drills, backhoes, cement mixers and heavy trucks, and more dust flies in the air.

This is all part of a scheme devised by European and US funders, a policy of anti-insurgency not dissimilar to that pursued in Northern Ireland. It aims at the creation of jobs to distract people and make them have a larger stake in economic development, so they realize that they would be harmed by strikes and resistance efforts. It is a sort of a shock absorber. It seems to have worked in Northern Ireland, thinks Blair, so why should it not in Palestine?

9 JULY

At one of the new Ramallah restaurants for dinner last night we saw an acquaintance in an expensive designer dress that must have cost a fortune. The restaurant had a well-laid-out garden, but I did not like the atmosphere. I am now concerned about the up-and-coming class living in our bubble with a most worrying sense of what constitutes trendiness. One male acquaintance boasted to another that he has a facial everywhere he goes. Always. And then many of the women (maybe the men too) have Botox injections.

This one has enlarged lips, that a smarter nose or puffier cheeks – it is grotesque.

The food at this restaurant was mediocre, even though every verbal attempt was made to promote and present it well. Needless to say, all these efforts were made in English. The menu offered 'Spanish ravioli'. The tabbouleh salad, traditionally most delicious with oil and lemon, was dressed in, of all things, pineapple sauce.

As we ate, a woman came around with cards asking us who we thought would win the football match being broadcast on the large-screen TV. She said they would pick one of the cards and the winner would 'get a shot'. We asked her of what, but she did not know. Even when we tried to get the waiters to use Arabic they would insist on replying in English. It was most bizarre.

The Palestinian Authority – i.e. Fatah – has cancelled the municipal elections which were to take place in July. Fatah could not get its act together and would have lost. The other candidates were able to make strong alliances and coalitions and had a better chance. Fatah didn't want the truth about their unpopularity to be revealed.

12 JULY

I was enjoying a recording of the Brahms Violin Concerto and getting carried away with the music when the telephone rang. At first the ringing blended with the music, but very soon I could not deny that it was the telephone.

I answered and heard a woman's voice saying, '*Shalom.*' Without thinking, I said, '*Shalom.*'

Then she began asking for Penny in Hebrew, which I can understand. Yet I found myself rudely blurting out, 'Can you not speak in a language other than Hebrew?'

She immediately shifted to English and I handed Penny the phone to hear a reminder of her dentist's appointment.

The music resumed after the phone conversation but I could not concentrate any more. I had lost my peace of mind.

Hearing Hebrew over the telephone aroused insecurity and fear, recalling earlier times when I received calls summoning me for interrogation by the military. So the automatic aggressive response is due to the arousal of my fighting spirit in the face of danger. But these are my own reactions, to be understood in the context of my own history, which was not communicated. On the other end of the line is a bored woman at a clinic. If she gets snapped at, 'Don't speak to me in Hebrew,' what is she to make of it? That the person answering the telephone is not clever enough to speak the language. So, right then, I'll speak in English. But she does not hear the anger and condemnation: the 'Do not defile my ears by bombarding me with your dirty language. I hate your assumption that the land is full of people like you, and only people like you, who naturally speak your language. You should know you are not alone here, that this is not your land alone. You are a usurper and should be kept in your place, and know your place, and not venture to make these terrible assumptions when you start the conversation speaking Hebrew.' Forty-three years on and I still find myself ranting at an Israeli dental assistant!

17 JULY

Out with our friends Alex and Maha, whom we hadn't seen for a while. Alex said that the last time he went through Ben Gurion Airport they made him strip and did a thorough search, even looking between his toes. He had a scratch on his head and they removed the plaster to look under it. In his soft, kind way Alex then asked the young man conducting the search, 'Why are you doing this?' The young man gave him the usual answer, 'Orders and security.' Still speaking gently, Alex said, 'For security there are machines to search the bags. Security cannot mean looking between my toes. I am as old as your father. Does it not embarrass you to do this?' The young man must have felt so bad that he ended up trying his best to help Alex, taking him through to the pilots' line for passport control so he would not have to wait.

Alex continued, 'I always considered myself a pacifist, have always been one. But after 2002 and the invasion of Ramallah something happened. Since then whenever I pass by a checkpoint and see them I cannot help myself. I feel a strong hatred towards them. Something changed. I know we cannot defeat them. We are not powerful enough. But there was a turning point. They are already on the downturn and will ultimately be defeated by forces within their own society. They have become greedy. So much free land to seize, more of it available for the taking, and why not? Who or what will stop them? America? The Arab states? Their conscience? Morality? Condemnation? Of course not. And the more they take, the more the anti-democratic forces in their society get entrenched and fight to keep what they took, the deeper is the rot and the faster the decline will be.'

18 JULY

Today Penny and I decided to take my nephew and niece, Aziz and Tala, aged eleven and fourteen, to the Old City of Jerusalem to visit the Haram al-Sharif, the religious compound that includes the Dome of the Rock and the al-Aqsa Mosque. I wanted them to be as proud as I am of the Islamic heritage of their country. Jerusalem, only sixteen kilometres south of Ramallah, is the site of one of the most attractive architectural treasures of Islam, the Umayyad-era Dome of the Rock. The Haram al-Sharif is third, in religious significance, behind the two mosques of Mecca and Medina.

I consider myself as shaped by an enduring Islamic-Christian culture that has been dominant in Palestine since the eighth century, when Byzantine Jerusalem came under Islamic rule. Indeed the Dome of the Rock combines Byzantine design and Islamic ornamentation.

Because of the Israeli occupation Jerusalem, the centre of the West Bank and the spiritual capital of Palestine, has been cut off and access to it restricted. It was not easy to gain admission to the Haram because Israeli guards at the door deny entrance to non-Muslims in the morning. But we eventually managed. After we joined the pilgrims, worshippers and idlers and made a tour of the place, we were approached by a suspicious Palestinian guard who proceeded to interrogate us, demanding to know whether we were Muslim or Christian. When we told him the truth he seemed offended: this was not our place. We argued that it did not matter what religion we followed. We are Palestinian Arabs and just as proud of our Muslim heritage as anyone. This seemed to infuriate him. He could not accept that the Haram was our heritage as well. We later received an apology from the director of the Awqaf [the Muslim Trust], but the incident was disturbing because it revealed a narrowing of outlook that seems to mark our times. Of course it was hardly surprising for the guard to be suspicious when the mount on which the Dome of the Rock rests is perhaps the most contested of holy sites. This Islamic masterpiece is plagued by Israeli state policies

The Dome of the Rock combines Byzantine design and Islamic ornamentation. I consider myself as shaped by an enduring Islamic–Christian culture that has been dominant in Palestine since the eighth century.

and threatened with destruction by extremist Jews. Yet I have always believed that our biggest challenge in the face of Israeli occupation is to guard against becoming a mirror image of our oppressors and adopting their ways and attitudes.

Then to dinner at the new house of Khalil and Samia, friends we had not seen in a while. Throughout the evening we made no mention of politics. The only reference was in a joke someone repeated:

An Israeli travels to London and has to answer some questions.
'Your name?'
'Shlomo.'
'Your age?'
'Fifty-two.'
'Occupation?'
'No, only tourism.'

We also spent part of the evening discussing the privileges some people enjoy, such as papers and ID cards, which afford one the greatest freedom of movement. Samia was concerned that with the Palestinian ID she had finally been able to get after a long struggle with the Israeli authorities, she had become imprisoned and unable to visit Jerusalem, or leave via Tel Aviv Airport. What is worse is that she cannot give it up: 'They do not respect my Italian passport. At the Israeli borders they only ask for it so that they can stamp it and restrict my visits to Arab countries.'

A man from Ramallah had better not fall in love with a Palestinian woman from Jerusalem, or Gaza, or Jordan, because they will never be able to get married and live together. Those with West Bank green identity cards have grounds for complaint. They envy the holders of the blue cards that Jerusalem residents hold; yet they also complain. A taxi driver who once drove me to a meeting put it very well. We were talking about what Israel has done to Jerusalem and he said, 'There is no *baraka* [blessing] in Jerusalem. Not in anything: not in children, not in money, not in houses. The Jews have made us lose any feeling of *baraka* in anything: *Ma feesh baraka.'*

19 JULY

I took the *service* [shared taxi, pronounced the French way] to the office this morning. Walking down from the last stop, I saw that the Grand Hotel gate looked as if it might be open. It was a hot day. The air was totally still and the sunlight seemed to be beaming straight down in white-hot, stifling rays. The only cool shaded place in Ramallah would be under the trees in the large garden of this lonely place that has been closed for the past twenty-eight years. I expected the main gate would in fact be locked and I would only be able to look at the garden through the picket fence. I was surprised to find it open. Maybe there had been some emergency and they had taken Aida, the proprietor, now in her late eighties, to the hospital, omitting to close the gate. Should I go in? I did.

Our old house was a few minutes' walk from the Grand Hotel, where my grandmother Julia used to spend most of her summer afternoons. I walked through the empty car park and into the driveway that circled around the first oval garden. I hadn't done this for a long time. I was looking carefully at everything to see what had become of the place. I could see that the garden was kept in top condition. There were no weeds and the bushes were healthy and in full flower. It was all arranged in more or less the same way I had known as a child. This is where I had played, studied for my exams as an adolescent and learned to love plants. It is the only part of Ramallah that has remained frozen in time.

I was so relieved to see that they had kept up the garden. Beneath the pine trees at the front were the asters that I remembered, the geraniums and the chrysanthemums. What I did not remember were the amaryllis. Not far from the edge of a raised circular bed were some lilies, their wide shiny green leaves spreading out like a fan, so unlike the dusty leaves of the chrysanthemums. Out of this profusion of greenery shot the most gorgeous bell-shaped flowers, with their variegated petals of orange, red and yellow. They were as exuberant and flamboyant as their owner, Aida, with her beautiful intelligent blue eyes, had once been.

She was the first woman in Ramallah to live a free life of work and travel and open liaisons with men. In the 1960s she had opened the first nightclub in Ramallah. It was called the Casino. There the Palestinian and Jordanian middle classes from the various cities came to dance to the music of the live band Aida brought from Italy every summer.

I walked across to see the state of the open-air dance floor. The metal grille gate was closed. I looked through. A single chair, one of those old-style wicker chairs with the rounded brown armrests, stood forlornly on the bandstand. Behind it I could see the door to one of the dressing rooms from which the performers would emerge. The perfectly round *piste de danse* in the centre of the Casino was still as I remembered it, light pink in colour with a smooth surface that was now covered by a thin scattering of pine needles. In one of the larger corner booths which used to be reserved for large groups, where the wrought-iron, pale-green tables and chairs used to be set, there were five

51

hens and a rooster who seemed to be taking note of this unusual occurrence, the arrival of a solitary guest at this long-abandoned nightclub. The rooster assumed the front position while the hens stood expectantly behind him. They remained solemnly in place, refusing to acknowledge my presence. It was a sad, eerie scene. My young friends and I used to go to the dance floor in the afternoon and mimic the trumpeter as he bent backwards and forwards blowing on his instrument. And we would peek into the dressing rooms where they disappeared between numbers. It was all so mysterious and magical, a whole world to discover which never ceased to fascinate us.

I couldn't enter that place without my heart thumping in excitement. It was here that I saw my first trapeze show, my first belly-dancer and my first magician. I never got to dance, though. By the time I attained the age when it was proper in conservative Ramallah for a young man to go out in the evening, the city had fallen under Israeli occupation.

What terrible timing on my part. I was born at the height of my parents' miseries and impoverishment in 1951, barely three years after the Nakba. The tension afflicting their life then affects me to this day. And this dance floor closed just as I turned sixteen and could have begun frequenting it, so I never got to dance and enjoy myself. I was stuck at home with a twenty-four-hour curfew just when I needed to be out experiencing life.

I walked further into the pine garden, where families used to sit to drink afternoon tea and savour those exquisite cakes baked by Aida. There, one midmorning, I saw my first yellow and black Monarch butterfly. I looked at the now dilapidated bandstand where the Italian musicians entertained us at weekends in the garden. As I stood there I could feel for a brief moment the shivers that went down my spine on those afternoons long ago when the band struck the first loud notes of their opening number, making this small pine forest quiver with the sound of their music. When I looked up at the balcony I remembered the yogi from India who was brought to dazzle us with the way he was able to twist his limbs, wrapping his legs around his neck. But because I was then suffering from stomach ailments, what fascinated me at the time was his ability to manipulate his stomach as though it had a life of its own. He would breathe out and leave a hollow space where the stomach was, or breathe in and his stomach would protrude in front of him like a basketball that was about to shoot out of his emaciated body. The day after I attended his show he looked down from his tiny bedroom balcony to where I was standing in the sun in front of the tall blooming dahlias. I squinted at the sun as I looked up and saw him there. He fixed his gaze on me. I froze in place. It was a penetrating look that went through my entire body. He seemed to be sizing me up, making me aware, as I had never before been aware of myself, as though I was looking at myself from the outside. It was the first time that I had had this sense of my entire being, standing there at the Grand Hotel in the strong sun surrounded by the flowers. I never forgot that moment.

But now I was brought back to the present silence, long and deep, amplified rather than broken by the low rustle of the wind passing through the pine needles – a sound I find most soothing. I remember that rustling sound from the many mornings spent in the grounds here studying for my university exams. I could stay listening to this comforting sound for hours. I walked around briefly and then heard the gate creaking shut. I was afraid I would be trapped in this dream palace of the past.

As I began to move out I saw where Grandmother Julia used to sit, in the shade of the lemon verbena in the early afternoon, at the table I used to be sent to early on to reserve for her. When Julia asked the waiter for tea, he would rush to the kitchen and call, 'One tea for Mrs Shehadeh.' And the kitchen staff would know how it had to be made: the cup would have to be filled with hot water to heat it, the tea had to be strong but not too strong and the milk had to be warmed. Otherwise the order would be refused and sent back. Later in the afternoon *Tata* [grandmother] would move to the table by the window of the dining room next to the hydrangea pot. That spot would be shaded because the sun had moved and it would be time for Madame Audeh, Aida's mother, to remove the curtain that had been drawn in the corner, where the hydrangea pots were placed to filter the direct sun from the shade-loving plants. There my grandmother would be joined by her friend Esther Jallad, who always came late because she first had to go to the movies. We all called this establishment *Outel* [Arabicised hotel] Audeh. Esther, who came from the coastal city of Jaffa, called it *Locanda*.

Now this entire generation of strong, eccentric women is gone. Gone too is their contemporary Madame Audeh, the owner of the hotel, who came from Lebanon, hence her talent at catering and cooking, which she passed on to her daughter, Aida. We always called her 'Madame', never anything else. And she always complained in a tearful breaking voice about everything: the business, the clientele, the mess they were making, or how their rowdy children were destroying the flowers. She would hold the hose to water her plants and then it would begin to shake as she started crying, the tears pouring from her eyes sometimes as abundantly as the water coming out of the hose.

e Grand Hotel with its lovely garden and night club. Esther Jallad is the second m the right in the bottom photograph.

Aida had done brilliantly at school and university and planned to work abroad, but she had to come back to help her brother with running the hotel. He was ambitious and in the early 1950s he built a new wing and the section where the casino stands, added a tennis court and wanted the place to be turned into a five-star hotel. He borrowed large sums of money to finance these grand schemes. But no sooner had he done this than he developed an aggressive cancer and within a few months was gone. Aida was left to fend alone, with a mother who was completely distraught by the untimely death of her son. Aida's sister was diagnosed with schizophrenia and had to be institutionalised in Bethlehem at the only psychiatric hospital in Palestine, where patients were not kept in the best of conditions. The mother spent most of her time in tears and Aida had to pick up the pieces and save the business. She worked very hard for many years, until by the early 1960s she had managed to pay off the debts. The place was flourishing. It had an excellent reputation and was patronised by people from all over. When the King of Jordan visited Ramallah, this was where he and his entourage would have lunch. But for an unmarried woman living alone with her mother, running an establishment like this, where alcoholic drinks were served, was no easy challenge. She had to cultivate her contacts and act with force and wisdom, which she did, managing to keep the place running at the highest standards. Then, the 1967 war began, shortly before her busy season. Ramallah was occupied. Just when things were beginning to get easier and she managed to make some money out of the business, another catastrophe struck. The Israeli army decided to make this their headquarters. They pushed Aida and her mother into one room and took the rest of the building for themselves. It was mainly through the efforts of my father, who intervened on behalf of Aida and her mother, that the army finally moved out. But the hotel was left in the usual mess that armies leave behind them.

Again Aida and her mother had to work hard to get the place going. But by then most of the middle classes, who had been the hotel's clientele, were gone, as were the guests who came from abroad. Those from the region could no longer visit and Aida suffered. She continued to run the hotel but it was not the same. No bands played music at night and the casino was permanently closed. The quiet that now prevailed was not comforting.

Then Joe, who is about fifteen years Aida's junior, appeared on the scene. The rumour was that he had come from the US to look for a bride. He was a friend of the family and was welcome to stay. When the hotel closed permanently, he was allowed to keep his room. Mother used to say he was like the guest who came to dinner and never left.

After the hotel closed Aida's mother, Madame Audeh, developed Alzheimer's and Aida had to take care of her. Joe proved to be a great help. He also introduced Aida to the Virgin Mary. She was Anglican but under his influence converted to Catholicism and began to attend Catholic Mass every day. 'Without the help of the Virgin I would not have been able to manage,' she once told me when we met in the street after her mother died. The mother thought that Joe, who had the same name as her deceased son, was indeed her son reincarnated and she grew extremely attached to him. Aida thought he was a godsend; the Virgin had sent Joe to save her and her mother. And he played the part and was a good companion.

After her mother died Aida, who had no close family members, kept the African violets, which Madame Audeh had particularly liked, in their place on the windowsill beside my grandmother's favourite table, taking care that they continued to bloom as they had during her mother's lifetime. She would say they were there for her mother's soul.

Like her mother, Aida loved plants and was a great gardener. She was good at whatever she put her mind to, whether it was cooking, gardening or running a hotel. In every way she was a capable woman who contributed to the happy memories of so many people.

I had finished my tour in this dream palace of the past and was about to slip out when I heard someone call my name. It was Joe. He and Aida appeared at the door of the main building. They were going to sit out in the sun and wanted me to join them.

At eighty-four Aida did not look very different from how I remembered her. Her strikingly blue eyes were still alive and her face was not too pinched. She wore a dark blue sweater and a blue skirt with a floral pattern. 'When she wears green her eyes become so green,' Joe whispered to me. He doted on her, standing nearby trying to see how he could make her more comfortable and help. He rushed to get me a chair so I could sit next to her. When I approached, she smiled and welcomed me with her eyes – she has not been able to speak since the stroke that afflicted her a few years ago – and wanted me to kiss her. I don't think I had ever kissed Aida Audeh before. And she held on to my hand and pressed it, wanting to keep touching it. She was sensuous and feeling. Then she began to cry, as her mother used to do, and Joe tried to stop her. He made sure to let me know that she had been spared the news of my mother's death, so I would not inadvertently divulge it.

I lingered on, trying to speak to Aida and comfort her, remarking on how well she looked, what a lovely garden she maintained, and how great it must be to sit out here in the sun. 'Yes,' said Joe, 'she gets bored inside and likes to sit out. It is good she can still stand on her feet. But she needs help. The stroke affected her hand and her speech. Her friend had one seven years ago and can now speak, but Aida cannot. It happened in 2008 and we were not quick enough to recognise it. The doctor then said it was Alzheimer's. But it isn't that at all.'

She hung on to my hand and I continued to think of pleasant things to say about how lovely she is and has always been, and how beautiful her garden was.

Then Aida put her hand on my head and managed to say, 'Bless you.' It took a great effort on her part to utter the words, but she did say them and I was glad to hear them, and to have seen her.

As I was leaving I took a last look at the garden. What a pity that Aida has made no arrangements to preserve it for the public after she goes. Who will get it? Perhaps she does not care. Would it be Joe? And what would he do with it? Divide it into small parcels and sell it and turn this open space, rich with memories for so many of us, the old-timers in this town, into a stifling jungle of high-rise monsters? She has no family heirs and I assume Joe will inherit her estate. But she must have known this. Whatever his motive, Joe has managed to keep everything in tip-top shape. And Aida has managed to stay in her house-hotel until the end being well looked after in her own home, even without a husband or children.

After seeing Aida in this state I wondered what would become of our house after Penny and I are gone. In *Howards End*, Forster writes, 'Houses have their own ways of dying, falling as variously as the generations of men, some with a tragic roar, some quietly, but to an after-life in the city of ghosts, while from others ... the spirit slips before the body perishes.'

All I can hope for is that the good spirit of our house persists as long as we're alive and that we enjoy what we've got as long as we can. I cannot hope for more.

21 JULY

Just back from a Popular Art Centre dance show in the grounds of the new Ramallah Cultural Palace. As we went in we were given information about the water crisis that is afflicting the West Bank. The show was dedicated to raising awareness of this problem. I arrived too late for the intro-ductory speeches but heard that the organisers had invited the families of political prisoners to attend the show without charge. And of course many of the songs and dances had a resistance theme, or promoted solidarity. On the whole the show was lively and there were some good dancers. I tried to imagine how prisoners' families would feel about this, and concluded that it was brilliant of the Popular Art Center to insist on dance as a way of resistance. There is something assertive, as well as uplifting, about dance, and we need it in times as dire as these.

As I looked at the easy and open interaction between the young men and women, I was reminded of how much of an outsider I was brought up to be and have remained. And what of those cumbersome trappings of grandeur which my parents brought with them from Jaffa, when the possibility of recreating their previous lives was gone. Wouldn't it have been better to integrate rather than continue to be a privi-leged outsider, aloof and distant?

Ramallah night-life is flourishing now that Israeli jeeps have stopped haunting the streets at night, making one think twice before leaving the house. With the extensive Palestinian police presence, it has also become as unlikely to be accosted by armed civilians in the streets as it is to have one's car stolen. While our security forces have a troubling record, the local police are doing a good job of keeping law and order. Many more police cars, donated by some European country or other, patrol the streets. Policemen are generally well behaved. They are now uniformed and equipped with radios. It was entirely different when Yasser Arafat was alive. He kept everything in flux and disorder reigned. This helped create the impression that Palestinian society was corrupt and undeserving of a state. Who would want to live in constant fear of having his car stolen? Better build a wall that keeps out the hooligans and makes it possible for us to live peacefully, thought the Israelis.

22 JULY

Just heard that the US Consulate has proudly announced that when Gazan students get a US scholarship, the US will drive them to the consulate in Jerusalem, keep them apart from others, deny them contact with anyone in the West Bank and then after they have their visa, drive them to the Allenby Bridge and to Jordan, observing the same rules of isolation. What an inversion of power, the US now acting as Israel's chauffeur!

Hadil Qazzaz, who works for PARC [Palestinian American Research Center], just stopped at our house for a visit. She is originally from Gaza and has not seen her sister, who still lives there, for the last five years. Knowing that her sister had won a Fulbright Scholarship and was being driven to the US Consulate in Jerusalem, she managed to get a permit and go to Jerusalem, hoping to see her there.

The smell following a shower of rain on dry earth has a name: petrichor, the essence of stone.

But they couldn't meet because her sister was isolated in a separate place away from the rest of the petitioners at the consulate, as per the agreement with Israel. This Hadil had not known. So her last resort was to go to the petrol station, hoping that when the 'drivers' – namely, the US personnel – 'escorting' her sister stopped for petrol she would be able to plead with them to allow her to see her sister. Fortunately for the sisters, this worked out and they had a short reunion at the petrol station as the cooperative consulate car was being filled up.

23 JULY

I have been meaning to go down the hill next to our house and save some of the coral fossils before the new road and building work catch up and crush them into smithereens. Today I finally did it. I collected as many as I could carry. My load was heavy. I had a rucksack with me which I filled completely, and on the way back I found a very attractive large stone which I also picked up and carried in my hand. I was panting as I hurried up the hill and who do I see but an acquaintance and his mother driving in their 4×4 to visit the site of their new building. They were bemused to see me.

'You need help?' they asked.

I showed them one of the stones I was carrying. 'Isn't it beautiful?'

'Nice,' my acquaintance said dismissively, without asking what it was, where it came from or why I was interested in it.

They were completely absorbed in adoring his child, whom the grandmother was carrying, the latest addition to a line of dull accepting people, driving down on an afternoon to check land they inherited from a father who inherited it from his, yet totally without curiosity or interest in the surroundings on the way.

I continued climbing with my bag of rocks, glad at what they probably saw as my eccentricities and wondering how they would report this 'sighting' to their family.

The not-so-common pyramidal orchid, which can sometimes be seen in the hills in spring, has migrated to my garden – for survival. It was driven away by the construction work in the area.

Perhaps I will leave the patch that used to be the lawn uncultivated, a refuge for the wild flowers that are chased down from the hills by the intensive building activity taking place there. And I might also display my collection of fossilised corals there too.

26 JULY

This morning when I looked at my face in the mirror I thought I was beginning to resemble my maternal grandfather, Salim. That grim serious expression, bespectacled eyes, the thin closed lips. Perhaps my grandfather came to mind because I was visiting his city, Jaffa, which he was forced to leave when he was younger than I am now, dying soon thereafter. Penny and I were heading to Tel Aviv to see an exhibition of the works of one of the earliest Palestinian photographers, Khalil Raad, and another exhibition of paintings, *Local Hero: The Image of the Arab in Israeli Painting*, and then to Jaffa for lunch by the sea.

Born in 1891, Khalil Raad lived until 1948, so his photographs are all of pre-Nakba Palestine under the British Mandate. A good number are of the port city of Jaffa, where my mother spent her first twenty-two years, the happiest days of her life. I took my time looking at the photos, trying to imagine what sort of life Mother had had in Jaffa, with its seaport and busy markets. I thought of her walking along these narrow, crowded streets, going to Tel Aviv or down to the sea for a swim.

After she died we found in the small cabinet next to her bed a handwritten diary in English covering the period 1944–5, when she was living in Jaffa and studying in Jerusalem at the English Girls' School in Rehavia, where she boarded, sharing a room with Jewish and Muslim friends. This is how the diary begins:

Saturday 1 January 1944
The year 1943 ended very cheerfully with a very big party for about 30 persons who included Salma Dajani and her husband. This party was intended for them on the occasion of their marriage … at the end of the party Deeb got drunk and we laughed at him. The party ended about 2 o'clock.
    I woke very late at about 9 o'clock still feeling very tired.

Sunday 2 January 1944
I got up at 8 o'clock dressed had breakfast and at 9 o'clock went to Mrs Salib and at 11.30 went to Tel Aviv. She bought a blouse for her mother and I bought a gray piece for [my] costume. It was Mrs Dajani who said that she is coming to take us to Tel Aviv. We dressed and went with her.

The Christmas break ended on Monday 10 January. Of that last Sunday she wrote:

At 12 o'clock we had lunch. After lunch went to Tel Aviv and I bought my red hood, changing my mind a hundred times at last when we walked a long way I decided to buy it.

We then went to the cinema and there Emile had a little fight with a Jew who wanted to stand in front of him. The film was called 'Random Harvest' at Cinema Orion.

The diary continues throughout the second term of the school year. On Tuesday 20 March my mother wrote:

All the boarders got up very excited for that was the day when we were to do the play.

In the afternoon we boarders did not go to school but prepared everything. At quarter past two the girls came in. Miss Barlow said the characters of the play are: Lucy Waheed, Miss March; Wedad Shehadeh, Beth; Tamara Cohen, Amy; Salwa Abdelhadi, Jo; Siham Shawa, Hanna the cook; and Najah Azzouni, Miss Crocker. All the girls laughed when they heard that Miss Crocker was Najah.

The play got on very well. The audience laughed very much. At the end we counted the money and found out that we had 14 pounds. Miss Barlow introduced Najah and Tamara to Pastor Nilson and then Salma and Najah presented him with the money. Everybody seemed to be very pleased.

In 1998, five years after the Oslo Accords were signed, my mother was invited by an Israeli film director, Esther Dar, to participate in a film to be called *Four Friends* which would bring together Salma Dajani, Sharona Aharon, Olga Belkind and my mother: the four girls who attended the same English Girls' School and boarded together. Salma

The Alhambra Cinema in Jaffa in 1937 which my mother used
to frequent as a young woman before the *Nakba*.

was brought from London, where she was living, the two Israeli women from Tel Aviv, and my mother from Ramallah. They all met at the American Colony Hotel, in Jerusalem, for the first time after nearly fifty years of separation. They visited their old haunts, the Girls' School in Rehavia and, for Salma and my mother, their respective homes in Jaffa, from which they were forced out in 1948. It was a bittersweet experience. Mother hesitated before accepting to take part in the film, but I encouraged her and she enjoyed the experience.

In the film there was an emotional scene in which Salma wept as she stood before the neglected tomb of her father, whom her mother had buried in the garden of the hospital he built and directed. As a counterpoint the director shot a scene with Olga and her brother looking in Tel Aviv for the house where they had once lived. This attempt at trivialising the Nakba by comparing it to losing a home through moving house destroyed the integrity and credibility of the film, and after the initial excitement my mother refused ever to see it again.

A year after Mother died, I got a call from Olga. Sharona had meanwhile died and Salma was not in good health.

'I've been calling your mother's number and not getting an answer. I tried several times. How is she?' Olga asked.

'My mother passed away,' I said.

'I'm shocked. When did this happen? Did she suffer?'

Then the daughter took the phone and said that her mother loved my mother and had a special relationship with her. 'I don't know if you were aware of this but I was. I too cared a lot about her. We were thinking of her and saying we should go visit Wedad.'

I remained silent.

She continued, 'We have your book and would like you

to come and visit. We live in Jaffa. Let me give you my cellphone. Did you write another book?'

After I put the phone down I thought of how mother would have reacted to her friend had she learned that Olga had moved to the city from which she had been exiled. I was sure my mother would have been gracious. She would have carried on a long telephone conversation with Olga, expressing no rancour. They would have chatted amicably and exchanged news. My mother managed to do as well as she could with her lot; it is I who, after her death, realize what she had to go through and find myself still angry at what she had to suffer.

It had all started so well for her. She had a dream life in Jaffa. Soon after graduating from school she married my father in what for years was described as one of the most memorable weddings ever seen in Jaffa, the beautiful wedding dress made by Dora, the many-layered wedding cake by Kapulski. The flower girls all wore white dresses and looked like seraphim. The photographs show the meticulous care with which everything was organised and prepared.

The young couple had hardly completed their third year in their new home with a new baby girl when they were forced out, leaving everything behind. It was the bombing of the *Saraya* [a Turkish word meaning the palace], which was then being used as an orphanage and was not far from where they lived, by the Jewish terrorists the Stern Gang, that made them decide it was too dangerous to stay. They drove the short distance to Ramallah, where they had a summer house, leaving Jaffa behind and the only quiet and happy period that mother ever knew in the course of her long but difficult and turbulent life.

Perhaps it had all been too good to last. Besides being

a successful judge, her father had managed to invest his money wisely, becoming the owner of a hotel on Nuzha Street, in one of the prosperous parts of the city. Her husband was one of the top lawyers in Jaffa. They were in a rapidly developing cosmopolitan city with huge ambitions and plans. They had a summer house in Ramallah for when they did not travel to Europe or Lebanon to spend the summer vacation. Then it was all gone and they were left destitute.

My mother would have been a prosperous woman. Instead she had to endure poverty and make do with little, with no prior experience of living from hand to mouth. The last pages of her diary are of budgets in *piastres* and shillings spent on milk and bread. We were brought up in one of the poorer quarters of Ramallah in a cold, draughty house that was almost impossible to heat.

Tragedy seemed never to leave her, steadily depriving her of all her comforts and the people she loved. Not only was her comfortable house in Jaffa and her husband's office taken away, but her father, perhaps broken by the trauma, suffered a heart attack and died in exile in Lebanon. To the end of her life she believed that had he been alive he would have been able to dissuade her husband from entering politics after the 1948 Nakba and complicating their life further. The judge had been like a father to his son-in-law, who had lost his own father early in life. The loss of her father also left her responsible for her difficult, selfish mother and this limited their options. At one point they considered emigrating to the US, but they could not leave her mother behind. Then her husband, my father, on whom she was dependent in every way, was murdered by a criminal encouraged by the lawlessness of Israeli military rule, leaving her a widow to fend for herself. 'All my life has been spent in one war after another, from the 1936 Revolt, to the 1948 war, to the 1967 occupation, to the Ramallah invasion of 2002,' she would often remark in her later years. When she was over eighty, the Israeli authorities refused to renew the visa of her helper, whom she loved and had come to depend on for her daily needs.

I watched the new, recently released film about mother's city called *Ajami*, which was shortlisted for the Oscars. It was painful to watch. Had it been set anywhere other than in Jaffa, it would have been a well-made film about drugs, murder, revenge and the horror of gang life, like similar films set in Mexico or Chicago. But it wasn't. It was set in present-day Jaffa.

What annoyed me about it were its ideological under-pinnings. Gritty as the film is, its silent script confirms the vision that Israel likes to project of itself as a country in the midst of a jungle, a dangerous region that justifies the militarism and murderous wars it periodically wages against its neighbours. The film portrays Arab men as noble savages given to hugging each other, evidencing how tender these cut-throat murderers can be with one another. When a gentle, slightly built and bespectacled Israeli neighbour approaches a group of Arabs to complain that the bleating of the sheep prevents him from sleeping at night (the film-makers seem unaware that sheep do not bleat at night), the men who are sitting around smoking *nergila* in the street, not only lack the decency to hear him out but have the effrontery to stab him to death. Simple. It's their way, that's who they are and how they normally behave as Arabs.

But the film did not stop at the Arabs in Israel. Those from the West Bank who smuggled themselves in to find work were also thieves and murderers. In another scene the missing soldier son of a Jewish family is found murdered with his watch stolen. A pathetically portrayed worker from the West Bank who has smuggled his way into Jaffa presents his Israeli employer with the dead man's watch as a gift.

All the suffering of Israeli Jews is caused by having to live next to the inhuman Arabs who are organised in gangs. Their justice is the justice of the *sulha* and traditional law. They live on the periphery, outside the norms of civilised Israel, and constitute a constant menace to the innocent members of that society.

But how did they come to live this life? What led to this and why are they so impoverished? On these matters the film is silent. Nothing is mentioned or even insinuated about the discrimination they face in society or the police brutality directed against them. No background is given, no context provided. No explanation of what the neighbourhood of Ajami was, or where those who now live there came from, and where the original inhabitants went and why. All of Israel's crimes are completely ignored and the only dirt that is portrayed is that of the Arabs. The viewer is left to believe that it is simply in the nature of Arabs to be thugs and hot-blooded murderers. The film offers no possibility of redemption or hope. Its subtext is that since the Arabs are so murderous, Israel is left with no choice but to oppress them and build a wall inside the West Bank to divide the civilised from the savage. Keep out the criminals and enable the peace-loving Israeli Jews to live their polite, cultured lives.

This film felt like the final insult to my parents' city, that same Jaffa that Ben-Gurion, Israel's first prime minister, wanted not only to destroy and depopulate by force, but also to deride. In a July 1936 diary entry he wrote, 'I would welcome the destruction of Jaffa, Port and city. Let it come, it would be for the better ... if Jaffa went to hell, I would not count myself among the mourners.' This film does precisely that to the city that was once crowned as the bride of the sea.

And Jaffa's ordeal is not over yet, now the inter-Israeli struggle between the religious and secular Zionists has moved to the central region of the country. One of the flashpoints is old Jaffa. According to the Jewish fanatics, it is the struggle with the Israelis for the central region of the country that has to be won. This is how the head of the Israeli left-wing party Meretz in the Tel Aviv–Jaffa municipal council put it: 'Very quietly without our noticing and under our noses, inflammatory core groups are strengthening their hold and fanning hostility and suspicion between the Jewish and Arab populations. I am not sure that the city's residents are aware of the move to Judaize Jaffa by Jewish settlers who undoubtedly consider themselves the successors of the generation of pioneers and those who drained the swamps.'

Two years ago Rabbi Eliyahu Mali left his home, his wife and nine children in the Israeli settlement of Beit El, next to Ramallah, to live in Ajami, the once 'posh' part of Jaffa. In an interview he gave, he explained that they had carried out a great project in the settlements for the past thirty years. With the Jewish presence in the territories already consolidated, the struggle now needed to be moved to a different place. Mali's new project in Ajami can be found in his lessons which are taped and posted on the Ateret Cohanim website. For example, in a lesson concerning the wars of Saul and their spiritual roots, he explains that 'there is a kingdom of preparation and a kingdom of eternity'. He then asks his students, 'You have no problem conquering the Temple Mount expelling the Waqf [the Muslim Trust] eliminating the Mosque of Omar and starting to build the Temple, right? But someone who lives in north Tel Aviv will say, "Are you off your rocker?" he will tell you that your irresponsible behavior is putting the whole of the Zionist enterprise at risk ... do you understand how they see it?' He then goes on to say that 'Forging the national consciousness is a slow, gradual process and before you reach the point at which the nation is with you, you have to go down to Tel Aviv. There is no other way.'

These fanatics believe that the struggle to defeat the Arabs is over. It has been won. Now the task at hand is to go after the secular Jews. Should I be relieved?

27 JULY

At the Institute of Jerusalem Studies in Ramallah I heard a lecture by Adil Manaa, the Palestinian historian from Israel, on the Nakba. As I sat listening once again to all the details of what happened, I wondered whether I would ever tire of hearing about and seeing films on 1948 and the Nakba. It is like Shahryar, the king in *A Thousand and One Nights* who can never tire of listening to Scheherazade. We continue to be bewildered and wonder how it could have happened, why it happened, how it can be explained and understood. We can never have enough of it.

Is it like the Holocaust to those Jews who were touched by it?

28 JULY

Last night we had Hassan, the father of our friend Rema, for dinner. He told us all about Jaffa's Rabitah. This is an organisation that is trying to make contact with and get assistance from Jaffa's present and former residents to save what is left of Arab Jaffa. Of the original inhabitants there are hardly 6,000 who are still living in Jaffa. But Hassan calculates that those who were forced to leave in 1948 must now have a million descendants. He is concerned with how to create contacts between them and those still living in the city. To me it seems an almost impossible task. To Hassan, the self-made man who was able to survive the loss of his family's fortune in Jaffa, nothing is impossible. Yet it must be easier for those who lost their homes and their property in Jaffa to think that the whole place is finished. To be reminded that descendants are still living there and holding on invalidates the image of an empty city in the minds of those who were forced to leave. Whatever was left was taken over by the Israeli authorities and is no longer theirs. Why, then, contribute to preserving anything of old Jaffa? It is the same as the tactic we employ when we lose someone we love: once we come to terms with the fact of their death, the finality of it makes the burden easier to bear. To have to think about the remnants of Arab life that continue to stir in the city is painful and makes the past harder to contend with. Nevertheless, I went with optimistic Hassan to Jaffa.

First we visited Gaby Abed, past president of Rabitah, whose wife is the principal of the Frères St Joseph College. He lived in Ajami in a typical middle-class house which he was able, after a long struggle, to buy back from the Israeli authorities, who had laid their hands on it. And what a house!

It was a period piece, a museum: an old Arab dwelling, preserved more or less as it had been, amid the dismal present-day reality. It must be one of the few remaining examples of how the houses of the Arab rich of Jaffa must have looked. It had the most beautiful floor tiles I have ever seen, a grand high ceiling and a long spacious sitting room with pointed arches, out of which radiated the other rooms. Perhaps not the best arrangement for the kind of life we now live, but very attractive interiors.

The Arab population of Jaffa, including newcomers from other surrounding cities and villages, is around 20,000. For most of them life is hard. Many live in dilapidated buildings they are not allowed to repair. The authorities use devious tactics: they prohibit residents from restoring any structure, then claim those structures are hazardous and must be surrendered. After that they take them over and renovate them. I was told that there are over 200 dwellings subject to judicial proceedings because they were built or renovated without a licence.

One of our guides was Omar Siksik, the current president of Rabitah, whose family owned the buildings in a main market street called after them. He pointed out one such structure now being renovated by the new Jewish owner after it was confiscated from the original residents on the grounds that it was unsafe and could not be renovated. In another case the staircase leading to an upper floor had collapsed due to disrepair, yet the owner could still not get permission to replace it. This meant that he could not go to the upper floor of his house. He found a brilliant solution. He brought metal stairs on wheels and placed them there. Since the stairs are on wheels and are not fixed to the ground no permit is required.

In the pre-1948 period Tel Aviv was built to contrast with Jaffa, which was seen as a filthy warren of crowded alleys. The new Jewish city had straight wide streets, open spaces and was dubbed the White City. Now the sorts of buildings in what is left of Jaffa's Ajami are in great demand and sell for huge sums. The city is being gentrified. The remaining Arab properties are being appropriated, renovated and sold to rich Jews, who would come to have the most superbly located buildings atop the cliff that overlooks the Mediterranean Sea, mansions that are superior to any that can be found in Tel Aviv. As we looked at such properties that have already been taken over and re-inhabited, I wondered how Hassan was feeling. When I asked, he spoke of his heart being torn apart when he sees Orthodox Jews, whom he called the foreigners, strutting with a proprietary air in areas he considers his old hometown.

On a wall at the Rabitah offices hung a 1949 photograph of Jaffa showing the wire fence that was constructed around Ajami to pen in the 2,900 residents who remained, like cattle. It was reminiscent of Jewish ghettoes in Nazi-occupied Europe. Father had tried to return to Jaffa. He first attempted to mobilise a mass return of all the people in Ramallah who had left their Jaffa homes a short while before. They held a meeting in Cinema Dunia and made plans to go back home. That night he received a threat from the Jordanian army and their plans were thwarted. This was in line with the policies of the provisional government of Israel as expressed by Ben-Gurion in a meeting a month after the conquest of Jaffa, when he stressed the importance of 'preventing the return' of Jaffa's Arab population. Father then went to Lausanne as a representative of the refugees to negotiate with Israel, but the representatives of the new state refused to talk, saying they only negotiated with other states. It was clear that Israel wanted the Palestinians out of the territory they had occupied. Perhaps by not returning we were spared what those Palestinians who stayed have had to endure.

We visited the Siksik Mosque, which was where the

77

Israeli Keter plastics factory operated until Omar managed to get them out. Now he is offering a huge amount of money to buy the *khan* adjacent to the mosque. According to Israeli law, religious sites cannot be confiscated, but the rest was taken. We were shown how this had once been the famous Siksik Market. I noticed other market streets that had also been named after a single family, such as Bistriss-Iskandar 'Awad and al-Balabseh. And yet some had been too stingy or negligent to register their orange groves fully, making it easier for Israel to get hold of their land. I saw just one grove that has survived in the midst of the cement structures called *shikunim*, built quickly after the establishment of Israel to house the early immigrants. Its owner had managed to stay in Jaffa and was able to reclaim it only because he had the registration documents to prove his ownership. The Siksiks had thousands of *dunams* of orange groves to the east of Jaffa. The land they owned was so extensive that you needed to ride on horseback to visit it all. It was taken over in its entirety and *shikunim*, those characterless cement boxes, were built on it. On the balcony of one I saw a shirt-sleeved old retiree sitting among empty crates looking perplexed and bored. Once this was where one of Jaffa's most famous orange groves had flourished.

The struggle is now reduced to the level of stubborn individual efforts. What can be saved, if anything can at all, is a piece here, a piece there. But the city of Jaffa, and what that city means to its million former inhabitants and owners, and their descendants, has gone forever.

I wondered how my life would have turned out had my family not been forced from Jaffa. I got an inkling simply by revealing to my Jaffa hosts that my family was originally from Ramallah, though they had been living in Jaffa and lost everything in the Nakba. I felt I was excluded by the others when we began discussing the agenda for our meetings with the Rabitah at the very first house we visited. I became the outsider who could not be included, who was not important enough to be a *Yaffawi*. Even after all that has happened, they remain so proud and hierarchical, still classifying people into those who are real *Yaffawis* and can belong and those who aren't and cannot.

Jaffa was a highly congested city, with narrow alleys bustling with activity. The café known as Kahwat el Tuyus [Café of the Imbeciles], which Omar had pointed out to me, was where the rich who had owned the orange groves but did not work them idled away their time, smoking and playing dominoes. There were six cinemas, a number of newspapers and clubs, but perhaps not much literary life. Had my family stayed in Jaffa I might have formed an attachment to the sea, which I now lack. I might have rebelled against the ways of the city people, the commercialism and materialism. But would I have been a writer?

15 SEPTEMBER

I came back from Scotland and found the garden looking miserable. So dry, so depleted. Just like the rest of the country, with its baked and wretched fields, desiccated and harsh.

So parched was the ground that when I watered it the earth seemed surprised at the unseasonable blessing, and I caught a whiff of that special smell that wafts up from the earth at the first rain. In *The Perfumier and the Stinkhorn* Richard Mabey writes that 'Natural smells are not just random chemical emissions. They're part of a complex messaging system between plant and plant, animal and plant.' How right he is! He also tells us that the smell following a shower of rain on dry earth has a name: petrichor, the essence of stone. '[I]t is all the things you imagine it to be. From fallen flower petals, flakes of oak-moss, pollens and resins and desiccated mushrooms, a huge ensemble of perfumed essences is washed into the ground and absorbed by porous stones and clay. When warm rain falls again, they're released back into the air to rekindle our memories of their ingredients.' I stood there after watering, relishing these complex fragrances.

Next year I am determined to concentrate on drought-resistant flowering shrubs that will keep some green and a little colour even if left on their own without water. I want to make a number of changes. In spring I will plant a few annuals. I will have beds around the olive trees in two levels, recreating the idea of terraced hills. I will plant cyclamen bulbs between the stones along these small walls and in the little beds plant red and orange nasturtiums that will hang down over the stones. Between them I will plant blue and white irises. I could well picture how it would look. My head was full of the lovely image of all the colours I will have in my garden this year, so that my eyes were already sparkling when I faced the immigration officer at Tel Aviv Airport on my way back. He stamped my passport and waved me through. Now I'm home again.

On my way out of Ben-Gurion to Edinburgh last month I noticed that the Airport Authority has planted an orange grove in the grounds outside the terminal. I wondered whether this was to lighten the ordeal passengers have to tolerate in passing through this airport. For me that endurance test starts at the outer precincts of the airport, at the external gate before the car parks. The guards manning this checkpoint are employees of a security company contracted by the Airport Authority. They are trained at profiling by listening to the driver and his passengers to determine from their accents whether they are Arab. Now, my driver told me, they have a device that scans the licence plate and displays the name of the owner. If the name is Arab, the driver is ordered to park on the side of the road. All the passengers are then asked to leave the car. They have to take out their luggage for the first of many checks before boarding the plane. I was surprised that they also examined our mobile phones. My driver explained that this is because they do not want the terrorist Arabs to be able to explode their cars by remote control. Having finished with this first trial, which can take from half an hour to one or even two hours, we were driven to the entrance of the terminal. Here we have to be careful not to attract the attention of the security officers in civilian clothing who guard the doors. We feel it is already an achievement when we finally make it inside the terminal and stand in line along with all the other passengers to wait for the main checking and search procedures.

It is important at this point to talk soothingly to oneself, to breathe slowly and deeply, and prepare for a long ordeal which can only be made worse if one reacts with anger, or reacts at all. This airport says it all. It has the look of modernity, with the security systems of which Israel is proud and which it promotes and sells throughout the world.

As we stood waiting our turn I could hear the exchange between two young Russian men and the Israeli official who had to decide what security category to tag on their passport. She ran through the usual set of questions that are always asked: the reason for your visit to Israel, who did you meet, did you see any Arabs, who packed your bags, and so on. Then, 'Can I ask you a personal question?' and before they could answer, 'Are you a couple?'

'No.'

'Then what is the relationship between you?'

'Friends.'

'But do you live together?'

'No.'

When our turn came we were given category number 6, high-risk, in Hebrew *shiesh*. I heard the brown-skinned man operating the X-ray machine into which our bags were fed calling to the woman who stood at the other end of the belt, 'Here comes the *shiesh*.'

We were tagged – not with any simple tag, but with one that is so tenaciously adhesive it is difficult to remove when all is over and done with at the other end of the world. It seems they want to keep you tagged wherever you might be.

I was beginning to envy those who got the number 3 and, even better still, 2. Then I looked down and saw a tag on my blazer. I was covered in tags, on my bags and even on my clothes.

As I watched how every item in our bags was removed, examined, prodded and probed, I thought of the first time I was subjected to this treatment at this same airport in 1971, when I was leaving for university. I became outraged that they were exposing all my private possessions and under-clothes and those of fellow women travellers to the public. But now as I watched I did not feel the same.

Then we were taken for a body check, where we were frisked. I was asked to drop my trousers. All the time I was remembering Alex's ordeal and wondering if I too would have the spaces between my toes searched. My belt, shoes and wallet were taken to be passed through yet another machine. But before taking the wallet the young man said, 'Give me the wallet, but first take out the money.'

'I will,' I said, then added sarcastically, 'not that I don't trust you.'

'I don't trust us,' he said.

The security person took us to the front of the line.

'Any good reason for this?' asked a British person annoyed at our being placed ahead of him in the queue.

Our chaperone gave a one-word answer: 'Security.'

Bedecked with *shieshes* as we were, and feeling rather like the Beast of the Apocalypse marked by the number 666, we finally made it to the line waiting to board the plane. I looked at the hand luggage the man in front of me was carrying and saw that it was tagged with a 1. Lucky bastard! I looked at him. He was tall, with a paunchy stomach. He looked like a South African Boer. How come he made it to 1? I was about to ask the fortunate fellow when I saw that he was carrying a Hebrew daily newspaper. He was of course an Israeli, a member of the superior race.

It is always when I'm on my way back to Israel that I feel most acutely how the Israelis are invaders who have taken over my country and closed its borders to the original inhabitants. We can leave and return only at the discretion of the invaders. The possibility of being refused entry at the border always looms large in my mind and keeps me on edge for the entire journey back. I realized that I was already checking my papers. For the past six weeks I have had a break from being hostage to my Israeli Identity Card, which at home I need to carry with me all the time. Obsessively I keep checking that I have not lost it, over and over, as though my life depended on it.

As I walked down the terminal at London's Heathrow

towards the gate for the Tel Aviv flight, I began to feel a kind of fatigue and loss of spirit, thinking of what lay ahead. I became aware that I was muttering to myself about how I should know by now that I cannot expect an early end to all this, so perhaps I should stop myself from indulging in my fantasies and prepare myself for facing the reality that awaits me on my return.

Then I saw them at the gate, the large-bellied men, pushing and shoving, blocking the aisle with their huge duty-free shopping bags, disregarding the queue, with long hair and fashionable sunglasses helping them to believe themselves Westerners to the core. Speaking loudly, thinking no one can understand their secret language, and perhaps not caring if they can, inhabiting a close and separate world. Among them I could detect a few sad and anxious Arab faces whom I joined, bidding farewell to equality and normalcy.

I tried to calm down, stoically bidding myself to accept my fate. Accept your fate, I told myself again. What is my fate? Perpetual shocks, delays, discrimination, closures, hardships and struggle. Anguish, bad news, lack of *baraka*, diminished pleasure in life; being held hostage to disgruntled officials applying regulations that keep on changing and you are never told. I know that the time will come when I will tell myself that I cannot afford to get angry, if for no other reason than for the sake of my weak heart. I will have to control my feelings and temper my emotions. I don't want to get to that stage and become like those old men who stand passively smiling and caring more about the state of their health and preserving themselves, as though they were all that mattered in the world. I want to continue to feel the anger and to *rage, rage against the dying of the light*.

I know that since I'm just back from Scotland I'm making an unfair comparison between our dry land and the green fields I left behind in that rainy place. In time I will adjust and will also stop seeing Ramallah as chaotic. Soon I'll get used to its jumbled architecture. I'll begin to look selectively, concentrating on what is good and attractive. This is the only way to survive here.

So many of the shrubs in the garden were covered with cobwebs that on this sunny morning are alight. I find them fascinating and can gaze at their intricate design for hours. But I had to decide whether to allow them to stay or remove them. They give the sense that the garden was abandoned, which I could not afford now that I was back.

I want to concentrate on the garden and make of it a small paradise, an oasis in this world of chaos and rude disruptions that we live in.

16 SEPTEMBER

One of the first people I met after my return was my good friend Mamdouh Aker, the Commissioner General of the Independent Commission for Human Rights, on which I also serve. He told me about the meeting he had chaired of community activists opposed to the resumption of negotiations with Israel as long as Israel continues building Jewish settlements on Palestinian land. As soon as they started, a large number of Palestinian Authority security officers in plain clothes, most of them young men, stood up and unfurled posters saying things like 'Mahmoud Abbas is the legitmate Authority' and 'We all support negotiations'. Loudly they chanted their slogans, preventing anyone from speaking. They were there to make sure the meeting could not proceed.

In his quiet, peaceful manner, Mamdouh tried to calm things down. He jokingly told one officer who was holding the picture of Abbas upside down that it is disrespectful to hold the President's picture the wrong way up. But his efforts to get the meeting going were in vain. People preferred to leave the hall rather than risk a confrontation, but the resilient Mamdouh stayed behind. Those who had called for the meeting went out to the street and began walking in the direction of the centre of town, towards the Manarah roundabout, where so many confrontations with Israeli soldiers have taken place over the years. But the protesters were not allowed to reach there. They were forcibly stopped by the police, who claimed they had no permit for a demonstration.

As I listened I felt the fear of a police state approaching.

7 OCTOBER

I am preparing an expert opinion for a long-standing case brought in the US against the Palestinian Authority for an exorbitant amount of compensation amounting to $116 million. The case is brought by the family of one Gaza settler with dual Israeli–US citizenship who lost their lives in 1996 as they were driving in Beit Shemesh in Israel in what was claimed to be a Hamas terrorist attack.

The lawyer representing the PA in the initial case claimed that it had immunity because it was a sovereign entity. Of course the US court refused this defence and ruled against the PA. The Rhode Island lawyer who was handling the case obtained a court order to freeze the US-based assets of the PA, limiting most economic and diplomatic activities in the US. As the governor of the Palestinian Monetary Authority (the PA's Central Bank) wrote to the court at the time, the freezing of the Authority's assets had forced a halt in all Palestinian dollar transactions through the US and could 'cause a banking crisis in the Palestinian territories'.

In my expert opinion, I pointed out that not only did the incident take place in an area outside the jurisdiction of the Palestinian Authority but the Israeli army had arrested the defendants while they were in the custody of the Palestinian Preventive Security Service personnel who were delivering them from Hebron to Nablus Prison. Also, the area south of Hebron, where the alleged attackers are said to have come from, is defined as Area B, where the Palestinian security forces have limited jurisdiction. Not only had Israel limited the ability of our forces to operate by preventing them from entering large areas in the West Bank, where law breakers could take refuge; they were now placing the responsibility for a killing that had taken place in Israel on them and punishing the entire Palestinian community by freezing the assets of the Authority in the US. Greedy settlers exploit the benefit of belonging to Israel by settling on Palestinian land while at the same time claiming the benefit of US law and its court system.

For distraction I turned to the online news. All of it was depressing. Israel is adamantly refusing to halt the expansion of its settlements. How is it that we are waiting to know whether or not the Israeli government would accept a two-month freeze on the settlements when the freeze is a no freeze to begin with? How can it be that a hundred years after the Balfour Declaration, when we are left with hardly 27 per cent of the original area of Palestine, we have to plead with Israel not to continue violating international law by building more settlements on our land as we negotiate an end to the conflict?

15 OCTOBER

Just back from attending the annual conference of Muwatin, the Palestinian Institute for the Study and Development of Democracy in Palestine. Founded in 1992, this is their sixteenth conference. The theme this time is new modalities for struggle. They offered a well-conceived programme, focusing on what they describe as an emergent Third Intifada. This is not localised here but is global and has features of civil resistance. I was glad to hear a paper by my old friend George Giacaman. He is Rita's brother, founder of Muwatin, and a professor of philosophy at Birzeit University. In his slow and measured manner (to accommodate the interpreters), he described the elements of a new Intifada that has already begun. Here was George after all these years still calling for resistance, for fighting the occupation that has dominated all his adult life, as it has mine. He is still trying to theorise, explain and lead. Admirable! After all these years we haven't given up. First a civilian struggle, then a militarised one and now global Boycotts, Divestment and Sanctions (BDS) and other non-violent means. We seem to have tried everything.

On returning home, I sat with Penny on the couch, the curtains over the French window to the east fully drawn. I was preparing a lecture on cartography to deliver to Birzeit students and the British Library. Penny was reading. We had tea. Our elderly cat was purring. The sun was setting. I was filled with contentment, working on what I chose to work on, trying to do the best job I could. We were warm in our house and outside the rain was providing needed sustenance. All was well with the world.

19 OCTOBER

Just been to a meeting with the PLO's Negotiations Support Unit, who wanted to discuss the legal aspects of land swaps with Israel. The morale and level of discussion were much lower than I remembered from past meetings. Many did not believe any real negotiations with Israel would happen any time soon. As I sat in the meeting, I realized how the bright young men and women I admired now look drab and rather pathetic, tired, not living up to their potential.

As we went on with the meaningless talk about the legal aspects of the negotiations that in all likelihood will not take place, it occurred to me that with every hostile action Israel commits in the West Bank it tarnishes its own image and grows uglier by the day. This was like the young man in Oscar Wilde's *The Picture of Dorian Gray*. Dorian is so in love with his own beauty that he does ugly things, and every time he does, scars mark his face, but he does not see them because he looks at the wrong mirror. He conceals his true face and continues to believe that he need never grow old, give up evil and settle into real society because he is different, special, enchanted and immortal. And how does it end? When Dorian stabs himself and the face turns into that of an old man, an ugly old face that shows signs of all the evil he committed in the course of his life.

Around 1979, when I used to defend cases at the Ramallah Military Court, I remember being impressed by the well-produced Israeli poster of 'Protected Plants', which had the names in Arabic and Hebrew, and photographs of wild flowers and herbs it was prohibited to pick. The poster was in a prominent place in the office of the secretary of the Israeli court, alongside another poster about kibbutz life, showing intellectual farmers taking a break to read a book.

During the long hours I spent waiting for the prosecutor and the judge to come so that we could proceed with my cases I would carefully study the poster. One day I noticed the young secretary in army uniform looking at me as I did so, but it didn't occur to me then how self-righteous it must have made her feel to be sitting right under this chart, proof if proof were needed of the superior standards of her people, who paid such attention to the preservation of nature. This was before the 250-plus settlements had wrought so much destruction on the landscape.

20 OCTOBER

During the period of the British Mandate Palestinians enjoyed a number of popular folk festivals that included the Nabi Rubin Festival in Jaffa, Nabi Musa at the outskirts of Jericho and Sitna Mariam in the Mount of Olives in Jerusalem. In time these came to be prohibited, restricted or gradually lost their significance and popularity until they dropped off the calendar. What was left was the olive picking season. Now even this is no longer festive and joyful but rather a struggle as Jewish settlers try to prevent the farmers from getting to their orchards to pick their olives.

21 OCTOBER

I saw George Giacaman today and he told me that he thought it is intolerable that the Palestinian security forces should be doing so much to protect the settlers while the Israeli security forces boast about wiping out the Hamas cell in the Hebron region with the help of the same Palestinian security forces. How could this be acceptable when our people have no one to protect them? The olive growers go to pick their olives and are attacked by settlers. They have no one to call upon: the Israeli police stand on the side, watching and doing nothing, and the Palestinian police are prohibited from interfering.

I had a meeting with human rights activists and one of them (S.) said that he feels something is about to break. When one side [he meant Hamas] is so harassed and attacked by the Fatah-dominated Palestinian Authority in addition to Israel, they are bound to hit back. Hamas is targeted mercilessly and they have begun to threaten retaliation. If they should strike back it will get very nasty, with inter-Palestinian fighting, and no one will be able to stop it. This is exactly what Israel wants and is actively provoking.

S. thought that until February of last year the Palestinian prime minister was responsible for the security services. He controlled the money. But then something happened and the power was taken from him – it is not clear by whom – and given to someone else in the Palestinian Authority. S. thinks that some shady character is now in control but is not sure who that might be. He says that the security forces exercise no restraint and have no respect for the rule of law. They show no mercy and do not treat the Palestinians who come under their remit with decency and respect. Such behaviour is very dangerous and could become entrenched and difficult to stop or reverse when the political situation changes.

Mustafa Barghouti, with whom I also spoke today, said he was concerned that should the negotiations resume and we turn into a Bantustan state, then the security forces would quell any opposition to such an outcome and we would be in a terrible condition. So he is strongly advocating immediate international recognition of a Palestinian state, and we take it from there. Not a bad policy as a precondition for starting negotiations with Israel.

22 OCTOBER

A clear blue sky, the temperature is slightly cooler and pleasant. It was olive-picking time for the three glorious trees in our garden. It is a good thing we have only three or my marriage with Penny would not have survived. Every morning I say: today we have to pick the olives. Penny has been pleading with me, saying that if I have to mention this subject could I not at least wait until after we have coffee?

Last year we invited my nephew and niece to help us with the picking. Afterwards they said it had been the most boring day in their lives. We have not repeated the invitation.

Walking home from the office a few days ago, I saw a woman I know and her son picking the olives in the fields next to their house. They worked in a joyless frenzy, with no help from the father, whose head is attached to his shoulders without the convenience of a neck. From what I know about him, he looks at the land belonging to his sister and hatches schemes for how to get his hands on it because she is childless and he fears it might go to the wrong people when she dies. The joy of living on the land, farming it and existing in harmony with it has gone. Land now means only investment and money as land prices keep on rising. The alienation, the forced exile from our land, even when we are still living on it, is more and more accentuated.

After we finished picking the olives, Penny and I took breakfast on the porch. Penny brought with her D. H. Lawrence's autumnal poem, '*The Ship of Death*', which we read aloud:

> Have you built your ship of death, O have you?
> O build your ship of death, for you will need it.

The grim frost is at hand, when the apples will fall
thick, almost thunderous, on the hardened earth.
And death is on the air like a smell of ashes!
Ah! Can't you smell it?
...

Oh build your ship of death, your little ark
and furnish it with food, with little cakes, and wine
for the dark flight down oblivion.

24 OCTOBER

Yesterday we went for a walk with our friend, the Palestinian photographer Bassam Almohor, ending in the village of Ajoul. We passed by the area where the new Palestinian city of Rawabi is to be established. When there are over a hundred villages around Ramallah, what is the point of establishing a new one? Why not expand existing ones, keeping the development in line with the contours of the hills? By acquiring land, chopping off the tops of hills and destroying the landscape, we are only mimicking the Israeli ways, which for decades we have been criticising.

We spoke to one landowner from Ajoul who doesn't like the new development and worries that they will destroy the spring from which he irrigates his small farm and grove. 'We have lived next to the settlement for forty years and have had no trouble from them. But these investors will destroy our life,' he said.

25 OCTOBER

Woke up early to a blue sky and delicious air. My cold is almost gone and Penny is playing a Bach fugue on the piano.

This is a particularly lovely time in Palestine. The

A view of our garden with the back porch. Penny and I are doing all we can to enjoy interludes of tranquillity.

temperature is moderate, white clouds are adrift in the blue sky, the air is dry and refreshing, the few hours of rainfall have washed away the summer dust and everything is beginning to prepare for winter, for rebirth again. I look around me and think how lovely life is, how dearly we should cherish and cling to it. And I think of Mother and wonder whether she was able to enjoy her last few years or whether she was too insecure, anxious and afraid of what was coming, too unhappy to be able to savour life. One must never think it is better to be dead. It is always better to be alive.

Penny and I are doing all we can to enjoy this interlude of tranquillity, taking pleasure in our house and the apparent security of life in it. No one bothers us; we wake up to beautiful mornings and greet the day looking out on the promise of garden.

And yet all around is uncertainty. There are strong fears that war might break out in Lebanon. Whenever Israel is coerced into negotiating a peace settlement, it finds a way out in a war that it either wages or encourages others to wage. Closer to home looms the possibility of civil war as the Palestinian Authority security forces put pressure on their rivals, the Hamas activists, arresting and torturing them. Calm and tranquillity – but for how long?

In the *London Review of Books* I read that Engels refused to live in the agony of historical expectation like his friend Marx. He relished the fallen present, deferring the rigours of salvation to the ever-receding future, where other people would have to endure them. Kierkegaard, Engels's classmate at the University of Berlin, summarised his objection to Hegel by comparing him to a man who, having constructed a grand palace, decides to live in a shed next door; the palace being the absolute future, the shed the existential present. Engels, one might say, did just the reverse. The Communist future would be an enormous shed; but till it came, he would enjoy the little palace of the present. In his will, after making a large bequest to Germany's Social Democratic Party, to advance the proletarian revolution, he went on to instruct the party leader, August Bebel, 'Drink a bottle of good wine on it. Do this in memory of me.'

This seems to have been Engels's solution to the problem of waiting out a dying world; I suppose I am trying to make it mine as well.

27 NOVEMBER

A few days ago there was a report in the Israeli daily *Ha'aretz* about how the settlers could not stand the smells of baking emanating from the Bedouin camp nearby. Today a young man came to fix our television and he reeked of a strong perfume. These days Palestinian men are fond of wearing perfumes, the stronger the better. This is because some sheikh, who must have a financial interest in perfume production, has declared that the Prophet Muhammad was fond of wearing perfumes too. He lived in the desert at a time when bathing was neither popular nor possible with the scarcity of water. Perfectly understandable, then, why he would be interested in people disguising their odours. Perhaps this is the solution to the settlers' predicament: give the Bedouins perfumes free of charge and make everyone happy.

28 NOVEMBER

This morning, on the local radio station, Ajyaal, I heard this story of a mouse.

> A mouse was found in the municipality of Bireh, Ramallah's twin town, wearing a ring with Hebrew lettering around its neck. It was deemed suspicious and was brought to the health authorities to be checked. The radio interviewer spoke to both the man who found it and the doctor in charge. The doctor, in an official voice, said, 'We summoned the mouse to the department for examination.' He was asked if he read what was inscribed on the mouse's collar. 'No,' he answered. 'Of course I cannot read Hebrew.' The interviewer pointed out that just as the settlers were populating our hills with wild boars, they might also be sending us mice that were diseased, and that was why the health official was summoning this mouse for examination.

Surely a most suspicious rodent! Either he was dispatched by the settlers to do us harm in as yet undiscovered ways or else he is a settler's pet that could no longer tolerate life in a settlement, so he escaped to seek freedom in the Palestinian ghetto.

1 DECEMBER

It appears from documents recently released by WikiLeaks that Israel wanted Hamas to take over in Gaza so it could wage a war on Gaza as a hostile state. Which is precisely what it did.

A group of brave and honest former Israeli soldiers have

formed a group called Breaking the Silence. This organisation has published testimonies by its members that reveal what they were made to do during their military service. In one such account the soldier describes how he forced a well-dressed man to leave his car when it was raining in order to humiliate him, and how glad his fellow soldiers were when he did this because until then he was acting kindly towards Palestinians. It was like an initiation rite which the soldier later seems to have regretted. Perhaps I was that Palestinian.

2 DECEMBER

I never forget this date, when the murder of my father twenty-five years ago changed my life forever. Last week news came of the death of a contemporary of his. What if he had been allowed to live out his natural life? How would my life have been different? Y.N.'s achievements were the establishment of what his family called 'a school for typing and shorthand' and travel agencies, for which he was awarded medals by various governments. He lived a good and, compared to my father's, a rather easy life, away from the annoying country of Palestine, to which he gave very little, if anything. Does it pay to mind only one's own lucrative business and not to be public-spirited? For sure. But would it be a fruitful and fulfilling life? Of this I'm not so sure.

How angry I become when I think of the way the Israeli police played along and were going to let me go in a car to Tel Aviv to follow the man who said he had information after we offered the reward, when they knew all along who was the murderer and kept quiet because it was convenient and served their propaganda purposes. How like pawns in their hands we were as they played with our emotions and lives, destroying Mother's and distressing me for so long.

This morning I looked in the mirror at the creases on my face. As I approach sixty, my resemblance to my father increases.

Walking in the old city later in the morning to get a plate of *hummus* for breakfast, I felt fit and energetic. I remembered Father starting early, feeling that despite his age he was young and vigorous, defying people's expectations. Now I realize that seventy-three, his age when he was killed, is not that old.

5 DECEMBER

I have just finished preparing for a book presentation at Ramallah's Franco-German Cultural Center. The two countries, with a centuries-long history of bitter enmity and seemingly endless wars, now share a cultural centre in Ramallah. The point should not pass without comment, when I make the presentation, that one day Jews and Arabs will go out to the world together as emissaries of peace, culture and renewal.

9 DECEMBER

Yesterday I had lunch with Mustafa Barghouti and Eyad Sarraj, the psychiatrist who lives in Gaza and founded the Gaza Community Mental Health Programme.

'What is it like living in Gaza these days?' I asked Eyad.

'At home I feel happy. I have a large house with a garden and a chalet by the sea. But once I leave the house I see all the misery and get so upset. When I have a good meal I thank God that I have enough to eat. So many have nothing.

Meat is something they hear of but can never have. Yet they manage. As refugees they always thought of that difficult day ahead and they saved. The women have their gold for dark days like these and they manage.'

He continued, 'In Gaza there's a lot of *amin* [security] but no *amaan* [safety]. The place is governed by forces who are not accountable to the government. When they closed the offices of the Independent Commission for Human Rights I called Prime Minister Haniyeh, but he was not aware of it at all. He later apologised. They came to take my sister's house. She left a while ago. The house is locked up. They decided they wanted it and just came to get it. I told them, even Israel did nothing like this, why are you behaving in this manner?

'But I believe Haniyeh would be amenable to something that brings everyone together. I spoke to the other prime minister, Fayyad, and we should have a meeting to try and restore unity.

'I was under a lot of pressure to leave before the war. We have British passports and the embassy was urging us to leave. My wife wanted to leave. I said, we will stay, even if the house is destroyed over our heads. I am so glad I stayed. Had I left I would never have come back. I would have lost myself and my dignity. Staying in Gaza has meant so much to me. It has given me so much strength to resist.'

As I listened to Eyad, I knew I felt exactly the same about being in Ramallah. Despite all the hardships, I've never regretted staying.

Then he went on, 'Haidar's house is now empty. His wife has moved to Amman. I used to walk by that house and see Haidar. He was the neighbourhood doctor. I looked up to him as an elder. It comforted me to see him, to know he was around. Now I pass by a vacant house. It is a very sad thing for me. No person comparable to him has remained.'

I thought of Dr Haidar Abdul Shafi and of our experience together in Washington, DC, during the negotiations when he led our delegation, and again in Scandinavia, where he, Mustafa Barghouti and I went on a tour to warn the heads of states there that the Oslo Accords would not work. I thought of how I felt about his warm paternal approach when we visited Oslo and met with young Palestinians living there. He was a man I would have liked to visit when he was ill, but I couldn't because of the closure of Gaza, and now he is gone. There is no reprieve. Never a second chance.

15 DECEMBER

Perhaps the whole project at the Khan Theatre in Jerusalem was doomed from the start, when I barked at that poor woman who greeted me at the top of the stairs and asked, in Hebrew, what I would like to drink. Instead of answering like a decent human being, I blasted away, 'Don't speak to me in Hebrew! Use Arabic or English, but not Hebrew.'

I was hot and tired from walking around looking for the theatre. It took much longer to find the place than I had expected. I knew it was near the old unused Ottoman railway station. I had been to it many times before. Yet somehow I went astray, walking up and down Bethlehem Road, asking bewildered passers-by for that century-old relic. I still call some of the roads in Jerusalem by their Mandate-period names, which I learned from my father. Shlomzion Street I call Princess Mary, and the German Colony, El Baq'a. I felt as though I was a time traveller, looking and asking passers-by for the Ottoman train station. Who would remember that? I passed the abandoned Anglican Church, so well positioned, with the copse of pine trees. The visual transformation that has taken place in West Jerusalem always stirs so much emotion. Then I found the place and was rudely awakened from my reveries by being addressed in Hebrew.

At the entrance I had met my old friend and Hebrew publisher, Yehuda Meltzer. We have known each other since the early 1980s. The last time he came to my house was over ten years ago and even then he had to be smuggled in. Israel has prohibited interaction between Israelis and Palestinians and has worked on keeping the two sides as far apart as possible. My good friend Naomi Eilan used to visit, then one evening I was driving her home and we were stopped by the army. They became suspicious, acting as though it was a crime for an Arab and a Jew to be together. This was as early as the 1980s. It has only become worse since then. Yet for those committed Israelis who want to visit Ramallah to see for themselves, it is still possible to do so. Nowadays young Arabs are beaten up in certain parts of the country if they have relations with Jewish girls, and an Arab man was charged with rape even when the relationship was consensual, but only because his girlfriend thought he was Jewish.

Yehuda's father was a Hebrew poet. As we were climbing the stairs together, I asked him, 'Why don't Israelis learn Arabic? It's one of the official languages of the country and Israel is in an Arabic-speaking region of the world.'

'You should see what the young people have done to their own language,' Yehuda answered. 'They speak a terribly distorted Hebrew.'

I didn't know precisely what he meant. His comment made me think of what the Palestinian novelist Anton Shammas, who writes in Hebrew, once said: 'What I'm trying to do [by writing] in Hebrew is to un-Jew the

Hebrew language to make it more Israeli and less Jewish, thus bringing it back to its Semitic origins, to its place ... As English is the language of those who speak it, so is Hebrew.'

My knowledge of Hebrew is basic, but even so I can recognise that something has happened to the language itself, not only to my relationship with it. It is pronounced to sound as distant as possible from the guttural origins it shares with Arabic. The teacher who taught me Hebrew could properly pronounce these guttural letters, but she pronounced them in class in the way a European would, to soften the sounds and presumably make the language easier. Then I didn't care. I saw nothing wrong in the Israeli attempt at being Western. I even thought of it as positive. I was not aware of the consequences this would have on our common future. Now I realize that in rejecting linguistic affiliation with the region and seeking acceptance as a Western state, Israel wants to forgo and deny the affinities its history and culture have with the region to which our two nations belong.

But why has the sound of this language become so offensive to me? Did the British and French feel this way about German after the Second World War? Were Chinese ears offended by Japanese sounds? Surely the Israelis can understand this aversion of mine, they who still boycott the music of Wagner.

It had all started so differently. I was keen on learning the language because I believed in the coexistence of our two nations. Now I cannot stand to hear Hebrew, which has become the language of interrogations, of summonses, for encounters with the military and of rude soldiers giving orders. After all that has happened between our two nations it is entirely the language of unhappy associations, of terrible experiences; not of decent human interaction, not

103

of culture and certainly not of anything that is progressive or good.

Ever since the artistic director of the Khan Theatre had contacted me a month earlier, I had been wondering why this project of dramatising my book about the 2002 Israeli army invasion of Ramallah, *When the Bulbul Stopped Singing*, had come up now, seven years after the book's first appearance in English and five after its publication in Hebrew? Yet late or not, no author would be unhappy to see his work presented on a stage – especially, in my case, for presentation to an Israeli public. It was a dream when I wrote the book that I would be able to hold the mirror up to their faces. And now here was the possibility that this would happen.

Attending the meeting to discuss the project was the assistant to the artistic director, who looked like the kind of person I would enjoy working with and befriending. She said she was going to do the adaptation and that the book had moved her deeply. She gave an example of a detail that she found so telling, the fact that of the two Palestinian policemen who came to the office in the beginning, one had dirty shoes and the other did not. But then she probably does not know how the situation has developed. How could she, when she had never visited or expressed any desire to. She indicated that she planned to present on stage a Palestinian who is like one of them in order to show Jerusalem's conservative public what this Palestinian had to endure. Immediately I worried that this could be patronising and problematic, unless I worked intensively with them to make sure it rang true.

I was curious why they did not want to use the successful script created by the Scottish playwright David Grieg. They explained that they were going to prepare their own, incorporating extracts from other books of mine also published in Hebrew. They did not specify which. I worried they might look for every conciliatory sentence I ever wrote, take it out of context and present me as a wimpy 'good Arab' to emphasise how even the 'good Arabs', who were not 'terrorists', were not spared. To work with them to get it right with my poor Hebrew would require tremendous effort and time, more than I could afford. Otherwise I would be unable to retain control over the material they used, culled from here and there, to produce the effect they wanted. I have no doubt that they would use only my own words, which would enable them to answer any criticism, even if they were taken out of context.

In the course of the conversation the director mentioned something about the Jewish settlement of Ariel and its cultural centre, which the Khan, among other Israeli cultural institutions, is boycotting. He thought that if the Khan were pressured, they would agree to present a play there but would insist that it be this one. They would then be forcing the settlers to see how the army treats Palestinians. The assumption was that the Ariel Center for the Performing Arts would refuse to present this play. But what if they didn't? I would never agree to have my play performed in the illegal West Bank settlement of Ariel.

What also surprised me was that they asked no questions about my current plight as a Palestinian living under occupation. No regrets, no empathy. How, then, could they create a credible portrait? In view of this, how could I trust them to portray the Palestinian in a way that would not embarrass me? If I had the time to work with them, I might be able to influence the course they decided to take. But I don't.

I feel more upset now than I did yesterday about their failure to ask me a single question about life in Ramallah, about which they know nothing yet still think they can present on stage. I also feel more certain that I'm being exploited in an inter-Israeli struggle. Theatre people in Israel have a problem with the settlement of Ariel. They want to use my work to fight their battle.

The biggest problem for me arose when we spoke of funding.

'Yes, of course we get funding from the Ministry of Culture,' they said. 'All cultural institutions in Israel get state funding.'

When I heard this I said I could not agree to have my play presented with funding from the Israeli government. This was absolutely out of the question as far as I was concerned.

'What if we find a private funder to sponsor the play?' they asked.

But then I would be deceiving myself. The state funds the running costs of the theatre, without which no play would be staged, I told them.

They then proposed that I could be spared the embarrassment by staying out of the picture. 'We will make the arrangements directly with your Israeli publisher, who has the rights to the Hebrew translation. What about that?'

Attempting to convince me to grant them the rights, they kept on repeating how important it was for their audience to see this play. I agreed, and this is why I publish my books in Israel. But the fact of having the play performed in a state-sponsored theatre speaks for itself and constitutes a clear violation of the boycott, which I firmly support. Having a stage adaptation of my book performed in Israel would surely be exploited in ways with which I would never be comfortable. The meeting ended without resolution. I needed a few more days to think about it and consult with Penny.

Before I left they took me on a tour of the theatre and showed me the hall where my play would be performed. I remembered being brought here by my father in the early days of the occupation when I attended a concert by Yehudi Menuhin, the kind, peace-loving musician who came to the Knesset and expressed his outrage at the Israeli government practices, its 'wasteful governing by fear, by contempt for the basic dignities of life, [its] steady asphyxiation of a dependent people'.

I did not get lost on the way out. Yehuda gave me a lift. As we passed the old Ottoman railway station, I wondered whether the trains would ever run as they once did on the old Hijaz railway, connecting Beirut with Haifa and Istanbul with Jerusalem and Nablus. Yehuda and I then went our separate ways, both perhaps dreaming of reviving those ancient routes and connections between the peoples of our region.

20 DECEMBER

I have just written to the people at the Khan to say that I refuse their proposal to dramatise my book.

This rejection has been more painful than I expected. It has brought home to me how far apart the two sides are. In the past I used to celebrate Seder at the homes of Israeli friends, yet here I am rejecting this offer to have my work presented to an Israeli public.

The Israelis have their own problems with their extremists and the settlers and are caught up in their own sense of victimhood, and we on our side feel vulnerable and suspicious, having so often in the past been cheated out of our inheritance. When I visited them in Jerusalem they gave no indication that they would want to visit me in Ramallah to see for themselves the actual setting in which the events of the book took place. We are no more than a twenty-minute drive by car from where they are in Jerusalem. Both the Scottish playwright David Grieg, who wrote the stage adaptation for the Traverse Theatre in Edinburgh, and Philip Howard, who directed it, visited from the UK and spent time in Ramallah before tackling the play.

1 JANUARY 2011

Spent the first day of the year swimming in the Arabian Gulf. I'm in Doha, Qatar, mainly to visit the outstanding Islamic Museum there and write a piece on a Persian miniature painting, *St Jerome Representing Melancholy*, an illustration from a Mughal royal album by Farrukh Beg, for a book on the museum edited by the novelist Ahdaf Soueif.

Not a bad way to welcome in the new year.

5 JANUARY

Just back from Amman, where I had lunch with Yusuf, an old friend of my father's. In 1965, just two years before the occupation, my father and Yusuf acquired a prime piece of land in East Jerusalem, not far from the Mount of Olives. After the occupation in 1967 the Israeli government expropriated large chunks of land in the eastern sector of the city, including the land they jointly owned. Years later that same plot was sold by the government and a new Hyatt Hotel was built on it. No compensation was ever paid. After we discussed the dim prospects of a legal challenge and even dimmer likelihood that an Israeli court would rule honestly in favour of Palestinians, we got on to a discussion of the chances of peace in our lifetime.

TRAVERSE THEATRE COMPANY present the world premiere of

When the Bulbul Stopped Singing by Raja Shehadeh

PREVIEWS Tue 3, Wed 4 Aug & Sat 7 Aug 2004
DATES Sun 8 - Sat 28 Aug 2004 (not Mondays)
TICKETS & INFORMATION 0131 228 1404 • www.traverse.co.uk

Both David Grieg, who wrote the stage adaptation of *When the Bulbul Stopped Singing* for the Traverse Theatre in Edinburgh and Philip Howard, who directed it, spent time in Ramallah before tackling the play.

I had not seen my father's friend in many years, not since his long ordeal during the Lebanese civil war, when he was running one of the famous hotels in the heart of West Beirut, where many of the journalists who reported on the war stayed.

When the Israeli army invaded Beirut in 1982 they came to his hotel and asked if he had any weapons. His answer surprised them. He said, 'Of course. Where do you think I'm living?' They took him away in their jeep and were going to shoot him, but the journalists alerted the international media and inquiries from all over the world reached the Israeli government. They started asking them- selves: 'Who is this guy? Better take him back.'

'When I got back to the hotel the journalists said we must immediately hold a press conference. I was asked, "What did they want with you?" I answered, "They wanted to know if I preferred *pastrami* to *basturma*." What could I say when they were still just a few yards away?'

He left Beirut only in 1983, eight years after the beginning of the civil war, and after the Israeli occupation of Beirut had ended. He had had enough. His faith in the Arab states was totally shattered: 'They give me no hope whatsoever.' He moved to London and did business all over the world. But now he has retired.

'Most men my age in Amman would go to their place of business and sit all day reading the newspaper. They find out who has died and spend their evenings at wakes, offering condolences. Death offers the best opportunity for socialising. I don't do this. I leave the dead to those who are only half alive. I never go anywhere. I live on a farm. I have chickens and deer. I cultivate fruit trees and vegetables. I never go to receptions. I work on my farm all day and would have nothing to say to the guests at such receptions. One time, though I broke my rule and went. Standing next to me I found the Israeli Ambassador to Jordan. After speaking a little he asked, "What would you do to me if you found me in a dark alley?"

'I'd put a bullet between your eyes,' I said.

'Then do you blame us?' he answered.

Yusuf turned to his wife, who had been silent all along, and told her, "This guy went to India in search of holiness. I want to go there. Maybe I'll find my Christ."

I understood the insinuation. Yusuf thought me hopelessly naïve. At this point I was reminded of my arguments with my uncle, who believes we do not have the military means to defeat Israel and cannot see there are other ways. I could never shake his deep pessimism. Eventually I realized it was a defence that he refuses to allow anyone to undermine. It was too painful for him to be reminded that there is still hope. As for me, even if it is folly to sustain our hope that Israel will be defeated and the occupation will end, I too prefer not to be disabused.

Between Yusuf and me there is a ten-year difference in age but also a world of difference in our experience of life. Would I grow cynical like him in a decade if no political change takes place? Perhaps.

Where we found agreement was over gardening. We are both compulsive pruners who have to be stopped once we get going at a shrub or tree before we destroy it. This is our way to drown our respective neuroses. Perhaps in our different ways we are both as extreme in our political views as well.

29 JANUARY

At long last there is hope. Lots of hope. Egypt has finally revolted. And a change in government would be a blow to Israel, which has so far been comfortably cushioned by the defeatist regimes along its borders. On all sides, and for a long time now, the possibility of a good life was restricted to only a small sector of the corrupt elite, and to hell with the rest of the population.

Yesterday, Friday, which the Egyptians declared their 'Day of Anger', I grew emotional, tears welling in my eyes as I read the *bayanat* [printed communiqués in leaflet form] which were being sent to the protesters, advising them how to protect themselves from tear gas and hold the lines. I was reminded of our own *bayanat*, issued by the National Unified Leadership of all the different factions during our First Intifada of December 1987.

There is much talk about what initiated the revolution in Egypt. It was smouldering for years, then the successful uprising in Tunis fanned it into flames.

Was it Facebook, Twitter, the Internet, mobile phones that made it possible to get it going? I have no doubt that all social media helped, but they were not indispensable. I know from my experience in the Palestinian Intifada that most important is the meeting of minds. What is essential is people's readiness, however diverse they are, to venture forward, to take risks, to defeat fear, to be ready to be reborn. In 1988 Palestinian civilians in the Occupied Territories rose up in mass protests against one of the most powerful armies in the world. I remember the way I used to feel reading those *bayanat*. It was uncanny how the words I read there expressed my own sentiments and thoughts. They matched so perfectly the pulse of the people that whatever these leaflets told us to do we were ready to comply. It was the first time that I understood the meaning of solidarity, the potential inherent in it and the power that is unleashed when people work together. An army as strong as Israel's could be held at bay when confronted by the iron will of masses of human beings determined to win their freedom. Those were scary yet magical times that I have never forgotten.

I watched television coverage of the young Egyptian men and women demonstrating in Tahrir Square, calling for the end of the Mubarak regime. I thought of my historian friend Saba, who is hardly squeamish, telling me a few months ago about the filth that covered Cairo when he last visited, the packets of decomposing food thrown in the streets on which stray cats and rats converged. This made me worried about the Egyptian people. By abandoning their public spaces, they must have been expressing a disturbing degree of self-hatred, and a loss of communal life and civic sense. Life in a congested city like Cairo is only possible because people have great tolerance and a high degree of that famous sense of humour that has kept Egypt going in the worst of times. Before the uprising it looked as if despair and demoralisation had hit so hard that all hope was lost. And there was the use of torture. It had become so common in Cairo that people had to cross the street when passing a police station to avoid hearing the screams. Everyone demonstrating today knows that they are breaking the Emergency Laws that have ruled Egypt for so long and that if they are arrested by the police they will be subjected to harsh prison conditions and share the fate of those whose cries make passers-by wince, walk faster and change course.

I am always moved to tears when I see people exposing themselves to great danger by marching for freedom. Isn't this what makes us human? We Palestinians have long been deprived of freedom, but we have not been deprived of our dignity. It is different for Egyptians, who are oppressed by one of their own, not by a coloniser as we are.

31 JANUARY

Our Egyptian friend Amer Shalakani writes in today's *Guardian*: 'America puts the security of Israel above the people of Egypt. We are monkeys to America. They are saying we Egyptians don't deserve political rights, don't deserve freedom. It's over ... the fact that the outside world continues to engage with this guy Mubarak is ridiculous. It's over.'

Several years ago I overheard two young businessmen, one from Tel Aviv, the other from Cairo.

'You should come and visit me in Tel Aviv,' the Israeli said. 'I will show you around my country. We can do fantastic business together.'

And the Egyptian replied, 'There is no reason why we cannot live together. We have so much in common and so many opportunities to make lots of money.'

'Yes, come, I will arrange everything,' the Israeli confirmed. 'It is so easy.'

I sat there cringing, my stomach turning. I am all for cooperation, for peace, for new times, for cross-border friendships. Why, then, was I feeling nauseous?

It was the callousness of these businessmen that distressed me: their lack of concern for the fate of the majority of Arabs; their refusal to recognise that over a million lived in the Gaza Strip in one large prison; and the way they ignored the fact that hundreds of thousands of Palestinians inside Israel and the Occupied Territories were denied permits to visit relatives they had not seen for years. Any chance of real peace had been usurped by this coalition of privilege and cynicism.

All day I have been trying to work, but I cannot tear myself away from the live TV coverage of events in Tahrir Square. It is so unusual for me to watch television during the day. It was inevitable that watching al-Jazeera and *Khabar Ajel* [Breaking News] would bring back the memory of those difficult months during the Israeli invasion of the spring of 2002, when we were besieged and had to follow the news all day long. Here I am now, watching television as millions did when we were under the sword. This time I am not enduring hardships or living in fear. But I can't help feeling guilty, lounging in a comfortable chair, feet up, nibbling nuts and sipping a drink while watching this live opera of a show. I wonder whether others felt guilty when they watched our travails?

2 FEBRUARY

We're witnessing a revolution in the making. It has revived my faith in humanity. How wrong I was when I gave up on the Egyptian people.

The Egyptian protesters on camera look as though they have been given makeovers. They look so much more handsome, with open faces, brave and bold, utterly human and alive, so unlike the way they looked for so long: defeated, despicable, disorderly. Now that the Egyptians are taking their fate into their own hands and fighting for freedom they are physically transformed.

Against these beautiful people the Mubarak regime sent camels, those unsuspecting beasts I've always admired.

I love watching them drink: they gulp, slurp and snort and then raise their heads after they've finished, assuming the most lofty, dignified pose. But when they charge they can be dangerous. After all, they have a long history of service in desert wars. They are huge undiscriminating juggernauts.

The sight of mounted camel drivers attacking the protesters is horrendous.

How many myths is this going to destroy? That Arabs cannot have democracy. That autocrats like Mubarak preserve the nation from the Muslim fundamentalists. That there will never be change in the Arab countries (Yemen is also flaring up). That Israel will always have its allies in the region and the Palestinians will remain under occupation. But of course it is also scary. Very scary.

Could the unhealthy polarisation we have experienced be a consequence of the policies of the autocrats? One Egyptian friend told me about her son's experience in Tahrir Square. Early on the secular and shaggy-haired Adam met a bearded member of the Islamist party. Ordinarily they would never have struck up a friendship. But thanks to the struggle in which they were both involved they were thrown together in a small space and became constant companions, spending all their days and nights together. It is revealing that Adam's new comrade told him, 'I would never have imagined I would be talking to someone with hair as long as yours.' To which Adam responded, 'Nor did I ever imagine befriending someone with a beard as long as yours.' They found that, despite appearances, they had much in common. They both cared passionately about their country, wanted an end to oppression and humiliation, and aspired to a future of dignity and freedom. Despite their different views on how Muslims should live, they were in no doubt that they could find a way to coexist and be tolerant of one another.

The Palestinian leadership, whether Fatah or Hamas, belongs to the class of Arab autocratic regimes. They see nothing wrong with those governments and wish to establish a state under similar rule. All demonstrations in support of Egypt have been restricted in both Ramallah and Gaza. How can we turn against a friend, thinks our leader, who supports the autocrat?

4 FEBRUARY

This Friday has been dubbed by the protesters the 'Day of Departure'. Giving names to the days is reminiscent of our experience during the First Intifada, which was an inspiration to many in the Arab world. It is most moving. Hundreds of thousands have gathered in Tahrir Square, chanting in one voice, 'Leave, leave. We will not leave until you do.'

This came after the Friday prayers, when most spectacularly tens of thousands of people had arranged themselves in neat rows and prayed with amazingly synchronised movements, raising their hands, bowing, standing, kneeling and prostrating themselves, sitting up and turning their heads to the right and left.

How can one not be heartened?

In the morning I went out for *foul* and *hummus* and at the bakery I saw one of those ugly Fatah people pronouncing to all who could hear, 'God help the Egyptians from those thugs the Muslim brotherhood and al-Jazeera, which is fomenting the trouble.'

A young man buying bread pointed out, 'Regardless, ordinary Egyptian men and women want liberation.'

'What liberation?' he sneered. 'They are destroying their society and will soon come to regret it and yearn for things the way they were.'

The man had no empathy for the people of Egypt, who were struggling to win their freedom from oppression. All he could see was his own fight with Hamas, which he believed would be undermined by the fall of Mubarak and the possible rise in the political power of the Muslim Brotherhood. Mubarak was the good friend of our enemy, Israel. Yet our leadership prefers him to the potential supporter of their local enemy, Hamas. This is what lies behind it. And al-Jazeera, of course, because of its sin of revealing the Palestine Papers [more than 1,600 confidential documents recording the Middle East peace talks with Israel and the US that were leaked to it] and speaking openly of the corruption of the Authority, is also the enemy.

There was a touching moment in Alexandria today when the Coptic Christians held hands to create a cordon to protect the Muslim worshippers from the police as they performed their Friday noon prayers. While this precious moment will not end sectarian strife, it is a beacon of hope for a long and difficult road. The Egyptians are writing the history of their liberation, with each Friday given a slogan like the title of a new chapter in the unfolding story.

For many years the Mubarak regime justified the repression of the Egyptian people on the grounds that Egypt was engaged in the struggle against Israel on our behalf. In fact, the autocratic Egyptian regime gave Israel some thirty years of false security and absence of real peace, enabling it to divert its resources to consolidating its hold on the West Bank and continuing to build Jewish settlements there.

7 FEBRUARY

Initially I wasn't going to go to the Human Rights Commission dinner, with some expert consultant who is paid a large amount to come from the other end of the world to evaluate our work. However, the director called and prevailed on me to attend. These days I am not so excited about institutional human rights work. Our institutions are falling hostage to the funders, who keep asking for 'deliverables', as if human rights are an industry. Anyway, some of the same countries funding this work are creating the instruments of its violation, the security forces and the organs of the security state. At the dinner one of the members of the Commission remarked, 'Imagine! Egypt has been selling its gas to Israel at a quarter of its market value. How could that be?'

At times of hope like this I find myself thinking of my father. He would have been ecstatic about the events in Egypt. But he would also have been worried. I too am worried. Out of habit I've learned to brace myself for the worst.

In Tahrir Square people are being so kind to each other, sharing food, telling jokes to keep their spirits up, making tea to sustain each other. How revolutions make for idyllic, romantic times.

9 FEBRUARY

Just been to a concert by the teachers of Al Kamandjati, a music school in the old city of Ramallah, established in 2002 with the aim of making music more accessible to Palestinian children, especially those living in refugee camps and villages. And then to the newly opened café, Beit Aneeseh, which was crowded with young people enjoying themselves. Why should they not live happily? Yet looming heavily over our heads is the occupation. How can we forget and go on with frivolous lives? How can we?

10 FEBRUARY

I was listening to the Beethoven violin and piano sonatas and writing, when our neighbour, Vera Tamari, called to say that the military in Egypt seem to have taken over.

We rushed to the television and heard the chants of the protesters in Tahrir Square (every country should have one): 'The army and the people are one.' I never thought I would be so excited by a military takeover, but the case of Egypt has been a difficult one. It was looking as though Mubarak would not leave, and the sinister head of security Omar Suleiman would turn everything around and save the regime. And he, who is Israel's choice, would subvert the Egyptian revolution and prevent real change from occurring. Apparently, he was personally involved in torture and overseeing the rendition of prisoners. There was news this morning that the Saudi king has told the US that if they stop the billion-dollar aid to punish Mubarak, his country would provide it instead to preserve the regime. Of course he would. Naturally he does not want to see a popular revolution, just as he did not want to see the victory of the Palestinian experiment in liberation and democracy and spoiled it by showering our leaders with money.

The al-Jazeera English coverage of the events has strong operatic elements. The way it is directed by the al-Jazeera crew is brilliant, like directing a live production. They talk to their reporters and analysts while in the background we hear the cries of the people. They then ask them to pause in the middle of this recitative and direct the camera to Tahrir

Square to allow us to see and hear the throb of history in the making. The people's chorus.

11 FEBRUARY

In the afternoon, taking a break from gardening and pruning rose bushes, I listened to the news. Then Penny called, 'The army command is issuing another *bayan*.' (How profoundly we react to *bayanat* after our involvement with them!)

A disappointment. The army is guaranteeing to the people (how can they?) that all the reforms Mubarak has promised will be implemented and, after the protests end, the state of emergency will be lifted and none of the protesters will be charged.

In the evening I was writing to Marina Lewycka when Penny called again. I rushed to the television. It was Omar Suleiman, looking grim and pained, as if he had just received a sound thrashing. A hawk of a man stood behind him. At first I couldn't catch what he was saying and thought it could only be bad news. But no, he said it: Mubarak has decided to leave and hand over the management of the country to the armed forces. The people have won. The people have actually won. Mubarak's regime has fallen after a revolution by the people of Egypt. It had taken just eighteen days of peaceful protest, bloodless except for those killed by his thugs.

A new age has begun. It was astounding: the joyful celebration, the euphoria of those who had struggled and won. 'Long live Egypt,' they cried when he left. Genuine joy and profound relief at the end of the Mubarak era. Next will be Libya, Yemen and Syria.

Something great has happened. Israel and the Saudi

rulers must be trembling and wondering, in the case of Israel, whether the peace it made with the tyrant regime will hold. All the assumptions they bet on have been proved false. The people have had their say.

12 FEBRUARY

Thousands of Egyptians have flooded into Tahrir Square to celebrate last night's ousting of Husni Mubarak, their country's dictator for thirty years. Many of the middle-class youth wore surgical masks and gloves as they swept the streets of the thick layer of dirt and dust. They pushed into piles the chunks of pavement that had broken under the weight of army tanks as well as the hammering of protesters making projectiles for self-defence. In large black plastic bags, they collected food and drink containers, old newspapers, empty cigarette packets and other remnants of the tent city sit-in. Other volunteers washed off or painted over the spontaneous graffiti that protesters had painted on buildings, pavements and bridges. Towards the end of the afternoon human chains formed to protect the kerbs that were receiving a fresh coat of paint. Hundreds of young people had turned out for what was called Tahrir Beautification Day.

After the 2002 invasion of Ramallah we also cleaned the streets. It was like a ritual cleansing to expunge the memory of the dirty operation that had come to an end.

13 FEBRUARY

This is the true end of the Sadat period, when Egyptian leaders (not Egypt) sold us cheap to make a cold peace with Israel. Israel gave back Sinai in return for continuing to build Jewish settlements in the West Bank and Gaza. But that fatal bargain did not bring prosperity to the Egyptians. For thirty years they grew poorer and more wretched. It only allowed Israel to free up resources for deployment on the West Bank. This is the price of making peace not with the people but with autocratic, authoritarian rulers. Now that Egypt is returning to the fold, where will Israel be?

In the Israeli media, the message conveyed to Hebrew-speaking audiences has been that the uprisings in the Arab world are no more than clashes between ethnic, religious or tribal groups and as such will have a minor impact on the villa that is Israel. This conceptual framework serves to underpin Israel's national policies with many of its neighbouring countries and with the Palestinians. It also fits well within the representational framework of the country as an island of civilisation surrounded by savages.

15 APRIL – NAKBA DAY

The Arab Spring has indeed emboldened Arab youth. Today thousands of Palestinian and Syrian youth marched from Syria to the border with the occupied Golan Heights. I was overwhelmed.

There is no denying the young marchers' immense courage, motivation and readiness to sacrifice. Thousands of Palestinians whose parents had been forced out of their country in 1948, along with Syrians whose parents had been forced out of the Golan Heights in 1967, marched to the Syrian-Israeli border, waving Palestinian flags and chanting, '*Esh-shaab ureed tahrir Filastin* [the people want the liberation of Palestine].' When they reached the fence, the Golani Arabs on the other side called out to them, 'Stop! Don't come any further! Mine fields – step back! Watch out for the mines! Mines! Enough, enough! Don't go any further!'

But nothing could stop them – not the fence, not the danger of mines, not Israeli guns. First they tried to bring down the wire fence with their hands, and when they couldn't, they climbed over it to the other side, where the mines were supposedly laid. As they landed on occupied Golani soil, those on the Israeli side began repeating, 'May God protect you!' No mines exploded; there were none. Everyone was stunned.

'This is liberation,' the Syrians living in the occupied Golan Heights said. For over four decades they had been deterred from crossing by what proved to be a flimsy wire fence and an area of combed earth which was supposed to be planted with mines but seems to have had none.

More than a hundred demonstrators crossed the border. One man, Hassan Hijazi, made it back to his parents' hometown of Jaffa and held a press conference before giving himself up to the Israeli police.

That there had been no mines at what had seemed like a formidable border for forty-four years was the most amazing revelation. Israel and Syria had convinced everyone of the impregnability of this border when all along, as these youths discovered today, one could walk across unharmed. The psychological barrier had proved more effective than any explosives, and once it was overcome no barrier was left. This is the most important lesson of the Arab Spring. Without vision we can never get anywhere. This is the first step.

Today I waited at the Kalandia crossing on my way back to Ramallah from Jerusalem. Driving past the high wall with the barbed wire which separates Arab homes and neighbourhoods from each other, I thought of that wire fence between Israel's occupied Golan Heights and Syria. There a fence, here a formidable wall.

Twilight had fallen. I relished the last glimpses of open space and a wide expanse of darkening sky. In crowded Ramallah even the sky appears narrower, not to speak of the skyline, which is so dreadful and distressing. There the Jerusalem sky was a beautiful colour, with a sliver of crescent moon. I used to love Jerusalem during the short twilight. I would take the shared taxi back, travelling along secondary roads, enjoying the light breeze through the open window and listening to the talk of my fellow passengers. How I miss the lost tenderness of Jerusalem. I would be completely carried away by the mellowness of everything around me: the narrow road, gently winding through the soft hills, and the pleasantly chatty friendliness of my travel companions. Now as we take the road back we have a four-metre-high concrete wall on our right. It was built right through the middle of the old road, separating Arab homes from neighbouring Arab homes as though a vicious enemy lived on the other side. It is topped with barbed wire where a number of soccer balls have been trapped.

I remember how Israel began to partition the road by placing dividers on the island in the middle while the traffic could still go both ways, as though to get us used to what was coming, to slowly habituate us to the pain. First one, then two dividers were placed in the middle of the road, then more, until they stretched along the entire length. I noticed them – how could I not? – yet still did not believe what was happening.

Now the wall is built and I still don't believe it. No trace of a pastoral mood remains; the atmosphere has become one of greed, bitterness and spite. Every day no fewer than 23,000 Palestinians pass through the Kalandia checkpoint. We are kept waiting for hours before we are allowed through.

As we waited for over an hour to pass through the bottleneck that had formed, with hundreds of cars crowding by the gate competing to edge their way through, I began to feel delirious. This conjured up a memory of Israeli Chief of Staff Rafael Eitan's statement that he wanted the Arabs to be like drugged cockroaches in a bottle. Has he perhaps succeeded, I wondered?

Staring at the wall that stretched ahead, I realized that it was not a barrier separating civilisation from savagery, as walls traditionally are intended to do. There was so much development behind the wall on the Ramallah side of the checkpoint that would now be prevented from connecting with its counterpart on the Jerusalem side south of this artificially created border. Surely this is what it is all about, a barrier intended to sever the natural continuity between Ramallah and Jerusalem, just like the Bethlehem section of the wall. Looking further afield to the east, I could see the Israeli settlement of Psagot, whose buildings were not blocked by a wall and were stretching to join, unobstructed, with the other settlements, creating a solid seam around the Arab part of East Jerusalem.

I once overheard two middle-aged Orthodox Jewish women talking as they soaked in the sulphur pool by the Dead Sea. They wore headscarves even while immersed in the water. One woman said she was only now 'making *aliyah* [Jewish immigration to Israel] from Australia'. Her companion boastfully retorted, 'I did it better. I came here forty years ago. My sons are in the army. No, we are not giving up any part of our land. God promised it to us. We have a small country.' It was as simple as that. They came, some early, some more recently, shoved us aside and now claim it all for themselves.

I was not unhappy to be leaving Jerusalem. I found myself agreeing with the tenth-century Arab traveller al-Makdisi when he described the city as 'a golden goblet full of scorpions'.

16 APRIL

Yesterday's events did not end without a heavy price. We have now learned that in the Golan Heights and south Lebanon fourteen unarmed civilians were killed and 112 injured by Israeli forces. Yet despite the heavy human price, it was a breakthrough. Walls and borders no longer appear as formidable and daunting as they did two days ago.

Among those injured in south Lebanon was a relative of mine, twenty-three-year-old Munib Masri, a student at the American University of Beirut. He was hit by a dumdum bullet, which is designed to enter the body and splinter, causing extensive damage. It was miraculous that he survived. It took a seven-hour surgical operation to clean out the debris, gunpowder and shrapnel that was left behind by the bullet. Both his left kidney and spleen had to be removed. The shrapnel that hit his spinal cord has left him paralysed from the waist down.

17 APRIL

I am intrigued by how the liberal Israeli paper *Ha'aretz* has been dealing with the events of Nakba Day, Independence Day for Israel, over the past three days.

After reporting the mass border crossing, they ran an interview with Salman Fakherldeen from Majdal Shams in the Golan Heights. 'The sight I saw amazed me and really brought tears to my eyes. Images flashed through my mind of refugees leaving their homes,' he told them. The reporter did not comment on how echoes of the past can be so strong for a man of fifty-seven, speaking of events that occurred in 1948, before he was born. But then, most likely to placate their readers, they ran a long piece entitled 'The Saga of Syrian Youth *Aliyah*', the 'heroic' tale of how some 1,300 Jewish children from Syria were 'smuggled' out of Syria to Palestine between 1945 and 1946. The children were separated from their parents. The story is mainly told through the words of Freda Ashkenazi, who was ten at the time. This is how she remembers the final day in the home of her parents in Halab [Aleppo]:

'I was convinced that we were going out on a trip. My father took me and a brother, Yitzhak, who was fourteen, and we travelled by train to Beirut. My father didn't tell us what the trip was about, and we didn't ask. We had respect for our father, and when he chose not to speak, we wouldn't ask questions.

'In Beirut, the three of us went to the city's largest synagogue. Our father sat down with us until the evening, and then some youth leaders from Eretz Israel, who spoke Arabic, arrived. They told us that we would soon climb aboard a big truck, and from this point on we couldn't talk.'

Fourteen years would pass before she would meet her parents again. She recalled 'being constantly homesick. I used to sit under a tree in the schoolyard, and wonder about what was going on at home in Halab. Bulgarian Jews on the *moshav* [cooperative farm] would call me, behind my back, in Ladino, the "Arab girl", but I understood everything they were saying. There was alienation and embarrassment about [my] origins.'

Freda later gave birth to four children, one of whom, Gabi Ashkenazi, became the nineteenth chief of staff of the Israeli army.

3 MAY

After a short but tiring book tour for the US edition of *A Rift in Time* my return journey was harrowing. I was on stand-by at Washington Dulles International Airport, waiting to hear whether I would get a seat on the plane, feeling utterly miserable at the prospect of spending another day in America. I had foolishly omitted to check in online ahead of time and Continental had overbooked. But then it worked out, though I was allocated a window seat with an obese man in the middle who used a CPAP [Continuous Positive Air Pressure] machine with tubes that made him look like an Indian elephant god. For nine hours I sat cramped in my seat next to this elephant of a man who was at least kind enough to apologise for his size and how he would be spilling over on to some of my space. 'Isn't it fortunate,' he had said when he arrived at his seat, 'that you are small rather than another fat man sitting next to me.'

Not untypically, the plane was full of Orthodox Jews. Before we took off a group of them prayed. One was in my cabin waiting for a seat and he joined the others from behind the partition. Three of them sat in front of me. One was a fresh-faced young man with his young wife. She occupied the toilet for the longest time. In fact so long that we were all worried that something might have happened to her. The flight attendant came and knocked on the door, trying to listen through it and asking if she was all right. She finally emerged to face the long queue of desperate people waiting to use one of five toilets shared by some fifty people in the cabin. She looked surprised when we asked whether she was OK.

Just as the plane was landing and we were told to remain seated and fasten our seat belts, her husband stood up and covered himself with his prayer shawl and began praying. The Orthodox live in a world of their own and follow their own rules. But I also suspected he was making a statement. They cannot need to pray so often in the midst of so many people. There must be an element of exhibitionism.

How true! [handwritten marginal note]

Before we landed Continental made us watch an absurd film about Israel and its claim to be a continuously existing state from thousands of years ago. The screen showed Bethlehem and other West Bank cities on the map of Greater Israel. Shameless! So there I was, ostensibly returning home, with the American airline carrying me there fully collaborating in brainwashing me and my fellow passengers into totally denying the existence of my country. What a welcome!

As we prepared to leave the plane I looked at the bearded face of the prayerful young man's companion. He looked exactly like what one imagines those ancient Hebrews must have looked like, except that he was changing the SIM card of his mobile phone.

When we arrived at the terminal the announcement was made and repeated that soon the siren would sound for the victims of the Holocaust and we were asked 'to respect the moment'. I decided to stop with the others. This completed the ideological package of Israel of the thousands of years and its establishment as the only way of overcoming future Holocausts.

13 May 2011

We left the airport and drove towards Ramallah, exiting the six-lane highway that only settlers can use and taking the unlit single-lane secondary road that turned and twisted through hills slashed by three roads: one for the settlers, one for Palestinians and one for the military vehicles patrolling the wall. At night the template of the land divided between settlers and Palestinians is clearly visible. All the roads used by the settlers are well marked and lit. Those used by Palestinians are dim and treacherous. Apartheid at its most blatant. Our poor hills.

6 MAY

It is Friday – no construction noise or dust, all quiet.

I'm at my desk in Ramallah, looking through the window at the olive trees laden with blossom, promising a good crop this year, with the nasturtiums, pink, red and yellow, cascading over the rocks below them. I am happy to be back with Penny, enjoying my house and garden.

I'm told our neighbour's German shepherd has run away. He must have had enough of being instructed in English to 'sit, sit,' in increasingly louder commands when he could never figure out what was happening, not having been trained in that or any other language.

13 MAY

After the ten o'clock news yesterday al-Jazeera Arabic showed a programme in two parts. In the first two men and a woman from Yemen were interviewed. For the first time I heard the voices of young Yemenis. They were determined to remain united and not to use weapons, even when the population is heavily armed. The young want to march to

Very soon it will be time for picking the olives from the trees in our garden. This year we will have a good crop.

the presidential palace and the old are worried about this. But they had a winsome way of speaking that endeared them to me and opened up another part of the Arab world that had been distant and closed.

The second segment was with two poets, one Egyptian and the other Tunisian, and an Egyptian literary critic. The Egyptian poet predicted that by 2017 there would be one united Arab world. How I admired him for this! He said that the enemies of the revolution in Egypt are many but the young will not let them succeed.

All this made me feel how much better life has become now that we have our own voice and our own Arab networks that present a different point of view. They do not focus only on the negative or put us on the defensive every time an Arab is interviewed. The Tunisian was inspiring, while the critic pointed out how important poets have been and how visionaries like Kawakibi* are now being vindicated and their poetry revived.

The young Egyptian was asked if he was distressed by the tension between Christians and Muslims, and he replied that he was optimistic. 'What we suffered under Mubarak was worse than anything that can happen. Now there is going to be change, development and unity. And it could not be otherwise.'

*Abd al-Rahman al-Kawakibi (1849–1902), a Syrian author who believed in Arab unity and solidarity, was one of the most prominent intellectuals of his time. His writings continue to be relevant to the issues of Islamic identity and Pan-Arabism.

24 MAY

In a scene reminiscent of the way the Syrian parliament responds to speeches by Assad, the members of the US Congress stood up and applauded Netanyahu when he gave the excuse (there are always excuses) for why Israel refuses to negotiate with the Palestinians. He asserted that Israel will not talk to a government that includes Hamas, which for the benefit of his mostly ignorant and gullible US audience he equated with al-Qaeda. So disappointing and sad to see all these venerable senators and members of Congress, with almost no exception, exhibiting the herd-like mentality of sheep, rising on their hind quarters and clapping their hooves for this inveterate warmonger.

It would be too boring to list and refute all the factual distortions (outright lies, in plain English – there surely is a legal term for lying to Congress, but just as surely it would not apply to an Israeli official) Netanyahu was able to put to his appreciative and uncritical audience. Here are just three. It is not true that there are 650,000 Israelis living beyond the 1967 lines. The figure for settlers living in the West Bank including East Jerusalem is 450,000. His claim that 'of the 300 million Arabs in the Middle East and North Africa, only Israel's Arab citizens enjoy real democratic rights' fails to take into account the discriminatory laws that apply to the non-Jewish citizens of Israel. And finally, he falsely claimed that he was 'nearly killed in a firefight inside the Suez Canal' in the 1970s, when at the time of the incident he was safely, and very likely comfortably, abroad.

26 MAY

I went to the post office to check whether the books I mailed myself from the US had arrived. Nothing. The clerk said that no mail has been delivered in over a month. When I asked him why, he said he thought it was because the Palestinian Authority was fed up with the delays Israel imposes on the mail and wants to direct it through Jordan instead. Later I found out that the real reason was financial. The Authority was refusing to cooperate with Israel as long as it withheld Palestine's share of the revenue from postage paid in the form of stamps at the point of origin.

We don't have a postcode. Yet many application forms require that you supply one. I have finally learned to write 0000 and this seems to work. Until we become a proper country we are the zero people, four times over.

5 JUNE

Unlike recent years, the forty-fourth anniversary of the occupation was not marked. Life went on as normally as possible under occupation. On my way to work I was driving by the newly remodelled Muqata'a, now serving as the headquarters of the Palestinian Authority. Over the years this Muqata'a had come to mean a lot to me. It was where the hated Israeli military governor of Ramallah established his headquarters. It was also the site of many of my legal battles, both in defence of security prisoners at the military court and in land cases, where I attempted to defeat the Israeli claim that plots fell into the category of public land and consequently belonged to the Jewish people. It was here that I first learned about torture. This was the place where many of my most formative experiences took place.

It was not until the January 1995 inauguration of Palestinian Authority rule that this compound was opened to the general public for a very brief time. There were many people solemnly walking through the interrogation rooms, the prison cells and the courtrooms. They were sometimes accompanied by former prisoners, who would point out significant markers – special spots, objects and graffiti on the walls – as they guided and explained. There was such euphoria then, and a sense of pride that the prison and torture chambers where so many had suffered had been liberated. In reverent silence we followed the former prisoners, who proudly guided us along the corridors of this labyrinthine structure, recounting what they had been put through. Sometimes the memory of one of those who died under torture or in prison would surface, and our guide would choke up and we would stand still, trying our best to imagine what none of us has had to endure. I was sure this place would eventually be turned into a museum, just like the prisons of Khayyam in south Lebanon and Robben Island in South Africa, after liberation.

I remember looking forward to the day when former detainees would accompany young Palestinians and describe to them the bitter history of our embattled nation. But it was not to be.

Of the old Tegart Building from the time of the British Mandate only the small area which Arafat had made his hideout during the 2002 invasion of Ramallah remains. It has been turned into a museum commemorating the hardship and sacrifices of our dead leader. Now the compound has high imposing walls with watchtowers. The old section where the military courts and the prison used to be has been completely levelled and in their place sits the new posh residence of the president of the Palestinian

Authority. The grand front garden is planted with palm trees with drooping heads bought from Israel. They rise out of a colourful ground display of petunias and other annuals in well-laid-out beds.

I slowed down as I approached the wall of Arafat's gleaming limestone mausoleum on the southern border of this lavish headquarters of our new self-governing authority. I wanted to examine a ceramic plaque embedded in the wall. It indicates the distance in kilometres to Jerusalem, the city Arafat had hoped would be the capital of the Palestinian state that has yet to materialise. I was startled by the siren of a police vehicle at the head of a procession of cars with blackened windows ferrying some high Palestinian official. They sped by, almost knocking my car off the road.

21 JUNE

These days the jacaranda and bougainvillea are glorious. The first will bloom only for another two weeks, the second will continue until December. On a recent walk in the hills I met a farmer who gave me an arboreal history of Palestine. He said, 'The earlier farmers planted olives and figs. Olives are the trees that last longest. They also had grapevines. They would dry the figs and grapes and eat them throughout the winter. Then when the British came they planted peach because they were in high demand and brought good money. Then with the orange groves in the coastal plain taken over by Israel, they planted citrus during Jordanian times. After the occupation, with the citrus from the coastal areas flooding the market, the price of oranges fell and we had to take down the trees. This was a big task. The tree has a layer of shallow roots near the ground and another web of roots deeper, some one metre down. It was very difficult to get them out. We didn't have bulldozers as they do today. We did it by hand. Then we started planting vegetables.' He showed me the fields of beans and okra which he had planted.

When he realized I was Christian, because I said I was originally from Ramallah, he let me know that the Christians always plant pomegranates. Why? Penny thought this was because the tree of original sin was a pomegranate, not an apple tree. Curious that even the choice of trees to plant is religious.

True to my origins, I have planted a pomegranate tree in my garden which is now in bloom. I suspect it's the tree whose roots blocked our drains. But the tree that is already heavy with fruit is the plum. It's drooping branches are redolent of the burdens of spring, the season of fertility.

I have now learned that *Eid es Salib*, the Feast of the Cross, which is celebrated by building bonfires to commemorate the day when emissaries of Helen, mother of the Byzantine emperor Constantine, found the cross on which Christ was crucified and lit bonfires as a way of alerting others to the find until the news reached the emperor, takes place on 14 September, when the pomegranates burst open like a cross.

Today I sat for a long time on my back porch overlooking the garden, with the dappled light coming through the gazebo covered with wisteria. It's been a lovely day, spent at home working on our book *Seeking Palestine: New Palestinian Writing on Exile and Home*, which I'm editing with Penny. The garden is just glorious, with colour everywhere, and plants hanging so naturally and looking as if they utterly belong there. I have finally learned what works best for my garden. I managed to plant cyclamen between the rocks that

Today I sat for a long time on my back porch overlooking the garden, with the dappled light coming through the gazebo covered with grapevines.

surround the raised earth around the trunks of the olive trees, and they're doing splendidly, sprouting out of the rocks like candles. The weather is superb, the whole place cooled by the gentlest breeze. The only sound throughout the day has been the chirping of birds. It started in full force early in the morning, when I woke up after a long night, having gone to bed all too early, and has not ceased. I want for nothing on a day like this.

How wise is Marcus Aurelius in his *Meditations*:

Men seek for seclusion in the wilderness, by the seashore, or in the mountains – a dream you have cherished only too fondly yourself. But such fancies are wholly unworthy of a philosopher, since at any moment you choose you can retire within yourself.

Nowhere can man find a quieter or more untroubled retreat than in his own soul; above all, he who possesses resources in himself, which he need only contemplate to secure immediate ease of mind – the ease that is but another word for a well-ordered spirit. Avail yourself often, then, of this retirement, and so continually renew yourself. Make your rules of life brief, yet so as to embrace the fundamentals; recurrence to them will then suffice to remove all vexations, and send you back without fretting to the duties to which you must return.

12 JULY

To a concert inaugurating a new concert hall at the Medical Relief Committees' headquarters in Bireh, near Ramallah. There was a performance by the Barenboim–Said Foundation's Young Palestine Chamber Orchestra. Some were very young musicians from Nazareth in Israel and various cities in the West Bank, Jerusalem, Bethlehem, Beit Sahour and Ramallah. Then there was Beethoven's Trio in C minor played by Barenboim at the piano, with the violinist Feras Machour and cellist, Mira Abu El Asal, playing extremely well. It was followed by Mozart's *Eine Kleine Nacht-musik*, played by the Chamber Orchestra with Barenboim conducting. And finally he played a Chopin Nocturne. The concert hall had superb acoustics and one felt embraced by the music. But, then, it had taken five years to get this hall to where it is now. An anonymous Palestinian philanthropist has contributed most of the money.

I don't usually enjoy going to concerts in Ramallah because the members of the audience are not attentive. Given how many children were in the audience, this one was relatively quiet. Except for the woman sitting next to me, who, as soon as Barenboim began conducting, followed suit. She began moving her hands excitedly and reaching out to those in front of her, smoothing the hair of the women in front without touching it and encouraging her young son to do the same. I wondered whether this was her tactic to engage him and keep him quiet or just her way of enjoying the music. It was distracting, but at least silent. I considered asking her to stop. I knew this would embarrass her and decided that as long as she and her young son were quiet I would let them be. After all, there are different ways of enjoying music. And Barenboim commands such respect and attention that even with this distraction I was able to concentrate.

I thought of the indomitable spirit of Barenboim, who said he would perform in Gaza and did. After the recital he told us that he had been performing for sixty-one years but had never received a better compliment than one he was given there. A man in Gaza told him it was very important that he came to perform here. When Barenboim asked why, the man answered, 'Because the world has forgotten us. Some send us food and medicine for which we are grateful, but animals also are given these. You have brought culture and reminded us that we are human beings.'

He said he was surprised by the number of young people in Gaza and their curiosity and desire to learn. 'The future of the region is in Gaza,' he said. 'If there is no justice for Gaza there will be no peace.'

He also talked of his relationship with the late Edward Said and said how important it was for him. 'I can hardly remember the time of my life before I met Edward. It was such an important relationship. We had daily communication. Edward had moral authority and was the best advocate for Palestinian rights.'

I thought of my father. How he would have enjoyed this. How he believed that so much could be done if the Palestinians and Israelis could cooperate to develop the two nations. Perhaps the timing was not right. Edward and Daniel began working together after the Oslo period, when there was a weakening of the PLO and it was possible to make headway. It was not possible when Father was trying his best with his projects, which in many ways were based on a similar vision.

13 JULY

All around lurks the growing danger of more frequent attacks by the Israeli settlers and army in the West Bank. The noose is tightening and still no hope of change. In his column in today's *Ha'aretz*, Doron Rosemblum describes it well. He writes that Israel's Arab Spring, which many had hoped for, had already begun, has indeed, not in Rabin

Square, but in the settlements: 'This is the pre-Zionist revolution seeking to systematically undermine Israeliness, to destroy the efforts to achieve a normal existence (codenamed "the national interest", "the rule of law" and "the diplomatic process").'

They are creating a theocracy with help from the highest earthly authority, the prime minister himself. So there is a new directive by the Education Ministry: starting this September, Jewish nursery and kindergarten teachers will be required to start each week with the raising of the Israeli flag and the singing of 'Hatikva', the Israeli national anthem.

The Nakba Law grants Israel's finance minister the power to cut the budget of state-funded bodies that openly reject Israel as a Jewish and democratic state, or observe Independence Day as a day of mourning. And there is the Boycott Law, which applies a series of sanctions on a person or organisation that calls for a boycott of Israel or of Israel's settlements.

And then there was the first reading of a bill to extend Israeli law over West Bank museums built by settlers that are situated in Israeli settlements. It has been described as aiming to strengthen Israeli sovereignty over the West Bank and to bring about an end to discrimination against settlers. Its author, member of Knesset Uri Ariel, said that 'the law must apply equally to all Israeli citizens anywhere without discriminating on the basis of political background'.

Interesting how he put it in terms of rights, when it involves colonisers who are depriving others of their land. How blind and ethnocentric.

14 JULY

Reading how the settlers are hurling insults at Israeli army officers made me realize that the tactics they used against us are now being used against other Israelis. This confirms what many predict: that if the Arabs stop being the enemy, the Israelis will be at each other's throats. In fact the internal struggle has begun, and this will eventually tear them apart. They commit a crime and then rush to complain, as in the Arabic saying *Darabni wa baka, sabaqani wa shtaka* [He struck me, yet he was the one who cried and went ahead of me to complain]. The settlers have burned hundreds of *dunams* of Palestinian olive orchards. When the army went to check, the settlers threw stones at them and are silencing any reporting of the incident. The Israeli army is constantly giving in to pressure from the extreme right. These are the same tactics the Zionist lobby uses in the US.

The settlers now claim that the division commander is prejudiced against them and has a leftist world view. They have compared him with Adolf Eichmann and are demonstrating with placards in front of his house. The strangest contradictory invectives can come out of the mouths of angry settlers.

15 JULY

In the *Guardian* of two weeks ago Tony Blair was quoted as saying that to ask Israel to give up Jerusalem is like asking Britain to give up Westminster to Germany. I think this alone should disqualify him from his post as the Quartet's special enjoy to the Middle East. With Blair heading the Quartet and Dennis Ross leading the US team, the chances for a negotiated peace are nil. As Akiva Eldar wrote in

Ha'artez, referring to Ross, if Obama really intended to justify his receipt of the Nobel Peace Prize, he would not have left the solution to the Israeli-Palestinian conflict in the hands of 'this whiz at the never-ending management of the conflict'.

16 JULY

The veteran Israeli journalist Gideon Levy reports that a disabled fifty-two–year-old Palestinian man on crutches applied to the Israeli Civil Administration to enter Israel for the ongoing medical treatment of injuries following a work accident there. His application was rejected. The reason for the rejection, he was told, was that 'no application was received in order to receive the permit under the terms of a security firm'. The rejection was accompanied by an oral explanation: he has to hire a private security man, at a cost of $200 an hour, to escort him from the moment he enters Israel until he leaves.

In another absurd development a case was recently instituted in Israel demanding that the Bedouins pay 1.8 million shekels for 'forcing' the authorities to demolish their village. Perhaps I should not be surprised. Do we not also subsidise the large prison of the West Bank to which Israel confines us by being forced to pay more than a hundred dollars in fees for the Israeli-issued permit to leave it?

Evidently we have not moved far from the logic of Golda Meir's statement when she said, 'When peace comes we will perhaps in time be able to forgive the Arabs for killing our sons, but it will be harder for us to forgive them for having forced us to kill their sons.'

17 JULY

I called Nihad Irshid, a colleague in Jerusalem, to consult over a case involving Israeli law.

While we were speaking he said, 'Let me call my brother on the other line. He is handling a similar case to yours. Let us see whether the court has reached a decision.'

As he spoke to his brother, I could hear that he immediately began using Hebrew. After he finished I commented on this. He explained, 'It is because this way the conversation goes more quickly. We're so used to Hebrew for the technical terms.' But then he immediately followed this explanation by praising the Israelis. He said, 'All the doctors on the Arab side write reports in English, while Israeli doctors use only Hebrew. They were able to develop their language to encompass technical terms but the Arabs failed in this.'

Hearing this made me realize how conflicted are many of the Palestinians living in Israel. The conversation ended when Nihad described Hebrew as 'the half-hour language'. When I asked him why, he said, 'Because in a matter of half an hour you reach the borders of this tiny state. You fly over the Mediterranean and then the language cannot be used.'

18 JULY

Went today to fix my laptop. As I waited I asked Farid how he was feeling about the Israelis he works with. He is a small man, always tidy and well groomed who, with his wire-rimmed glasses, looks like a bright student. He speaks slowly, enunciating every word. Because he buys his computers from an Israeli agent, he is among those businessmen who get special permits to cross into Israel. This privilege is also conferred on those involved in the security forces and officials of the Palestinian Authority. A special section of the Oslo Accords is titled 'Passage of VIPs' and enumerates the privileges to which holders of the VIP card issued by Israel are entitled. The sight of those stranded at checkpoints while others pass through the first-class lanes or go through checkpoints without searches – these became jarring common sights that destroyed our spirit from within, depriving us of our dignity and the values we had long cherished.

I still remember how in 2003, during the Second Intifada, when he was working in our house, Farid had described the Israelis as subhuman. This is what he told me then: 'If the Israelis think it will all end by getting rid of us they are mistaken. I will not leave even if I have to eat grass, even if I have to live in a tent. Despite the checkpoints I go on working. I have to pay for the education of my brother, for my wife and children, for my father. We would send someone across the checkpoint with empty bags. Then they would return with the computers, carrying as many as possible. We would go back and forth, carrying these heavy machines by hand. We would come home so exhausted, all we could do was sleep. Sometimes they would not allow the van in, sometimes they would. Purely on a whim. Sometimes they would say: "Take everything out." In the rain, the machines would have to be removed. And sometimes they would smash the computer screens. We lost so many. We lost them. That was it. They could not be repaired. We simply lost them. Yet still every house has a computer now, even those in the remote villages. The labourers come to me with their sons. I can read their character from what they ask for. "I want shooting with guns." "I want it with blood," one boy would say, and another would say: "I want something about space" or "I want to learn about animals." This gives me a clue of the kind of home they come from. A *fellah* [farmer] also comes. They come to town with their produce, sell it and go back with the belt of money round their waist. I know them. They would take the money and say: "We want you to advise us on what computer to buy." Some people cheat them. I have never cheated anyone like this. I don't want to brag about myself, but I always help them. If I can give them anything for free I do. I think it is an insult to humanity to call the Jews humans. They are worse than cows. If they knew how much we hated them they would not stay. We are willing for our children to die so that they could be hurt.'

'Is this what you think?' I asked him.

'This is what people generally think,' he answered.

Now he was rather more nuanced in his assessment of the Israelis. 'They love money and will do anything for money,' he said. Choosing his words carefully, he told me: 'They also have a strong hatred of us and lump us all in one group and would rather be rid of us. Their feelings get the better of them.' This, he thought, 'would mean it will be difficult for them to adjust to their surroundings, since they also have a demographic problem with the Arabs, who will soon become a majority. And being discontented and an underclass, the Arabs cannot be kept down forever.'

He also thought that they had a low level of tolerance: 'Once there is uncertainty and fear, like when the rockets fell two years ago and business was affected for a long time. This is because they come from different countries. They are not like us, with a high level of resilience. Israel is supposed to be heaven and if it does not live up to this, then they are not willing to put up with it.'

When I thought about what he said I felt he had got it right. Our resilience does indeed arise out of our being more homogeneous. Ours is the more closely knit society, whereas theirs is composed of Jews from different parts of the world. In this sense it is more of a shaky construct. This might explain why I feel that knot in my gut when I hear of their plans for new regulations for the gates through which we can enter our walled enclaves or for an extension of the annexation wall or the different ways they're devising to confine and control us. Given the nature of their society, it comes more naturally to them that they need to draw up long-term strategies to preserve their cohesiveness and control over us. Or at least so they believe.

Israel is like a corporation with highly planned sectors, such as the army and the Land Authority that controls over 90 per cent of the land in Israel. Like a corporation, if the management is ineffective, or fails, the future becomes bleak. Things are not going well in Israel with a misguided leadership at the helm.

Amira Hass, the courageous Israeli journalist who for a number of years has been living in Ramallah, expressed to me her disappointment that Palestinians are willing to interact (sometimes even on a friendly basis) with former members of the Israeli military government and of Shabak [Israeli security forces] who after retirement work as businessmen and yet they boycott Israelis active in the solidarity movement. I agreed with her that this is shameful behaviour.

19 JULY

I went to get a haircut at Hinn's. His shop is directly opposite where Cinema Dunia used to be before it was demolished and a new monstrosity now, called the Dunia Trade Center, was put in its place. It was there that the Palestinian refugees from Jaffa, Lydda and Ramle met in 1948 and decided to go back to the homes they had left a short while ago. My father was one of those behind the initiative. Among the refugees present at the meeting was Habib, the father of Iskandar Hinn, who now cuts my hair. He died several years ago and his photograph, with a forced smile, adorns the wall. All along Main Street in Ramallah are shops with pictures on the wall facing the door of deceased fathers who established these stores and left them for their children. Many of them had stores in Jaffa. Habib had been my father's barber in Jaffa. His shop was just around the corner from the court, so my father would stop on his way to get a haircut or a shave. He continued to cut my father's hair in Ramallah until Father was killed. Now his sons are my barbers and have been all my life.

Habib and the other refugees met in Cinema Dunia and decided to return en masse to their homes. The road was open, so why not? But they were stopped by the Arab Legion, with its British commander, Glubb Pasha, who persisted in doing his best to halt infiltration into Israel and to prevent border incidents. Then they elected a secretariat, my father among them, to represent the refugees in Lausanne, where father travelled, only to be disappointed by Israel's refusal to engage with them.

But all this happened before I was born.

The Cinema Dunia I remember was a happier place where many movies were shown. One of its best customers was Esther Jallad, my grandmother's friend. Whenever I think of Esther I think of Cinema Dunia, one of three movie houses in Ramallah, all of which are now closed.

She and her family were expelled from their opulent

150

Cinema Dunia in its heyday, one of three cinemas in Ramallah before the Israeli occupation in 1967, and favoured by my grandmother's friend, Ester Jallad.

home in the port city of Jaffa in 1948 and found themselves in the hilly town of Ramallah. In her displacement, Esther carried one passion with her: she loved to go to the movies. Conveniently, she lived just up the hill from Cinema Dunia. Every afternoon at three-fifteen, dressed to the hilt, her pursed mouth heavily lipsticked, eyelids smudged with pink eyeshadow, her large handbag dangling from her crooked arm, she would walk down from her house to the cinema as though on a rendezvous that could never be missed. The cinema had three classes of seats: stalls (the cheapest), the dress circle and the *balkon* (balcony or box seats). One of the six *balkons* in the cinema was reserved for her. Everyone knew it was Madame Jallad's box and whenever we went to the Cinema Dunia we never failed to see Esther, with her head cocked, occupying one of the four upholstered chairs that were fitted in each of the *balkons*, a lone figure quietly concentrating on the film being projected on the wide screen.

Two films were shown in the afternoon, starting at three-thirty, one *ajnabi* (foreign) and the other an Arabic film. Almost always the *ajnabi* was in English; very rarely were French films shown, unless they featured Brigitte Bardot. The show began with the Jordanian national anthem, to which we rose from our seats, with the exception of Esther, who never did. Once I tried to follow her example, only to have the usher flash his light at me slumped in the seat, displaying disrespect to our king, whose image standing before the flag filled the screen. The Arabic films were Egyptian and were good. The *ajnabi* movies that made their way to Ramallah were a mish-mash. It was not a free choice for the cinema manager, because he was restricted by both the censor – who had to approve every movie – and the availability of movies provided by distributors in Cairo and Beirut, who added Arabic subtitles to the films they marketed throughout the Arab world.

Esther's command of English was limited and she was too near-sighted to read subtitles comfortably. French was her second language, a marker of sophistication among the higher classes of Jaffa. What did Esther make of the films she watched? She never discussed them, never spoke about what she saw. Her movie-going was a solemnly solitary affair.

Then, on the cursed day of 6 June 1967, Israel occupied the West Bank and we were cut off from the Arab world and from the film distributors who supplied films to the cinemas in the West Bank. After a few months Cinema Dunia, along with the other two movie houses in Ramallah, Jameel and Walid, and all three in Arab East Jerusalem, closed down. Occupation and entertainment did not go together. For many years the billboard outside Cinema Dunia showed the same advertisement for the last film that was screened there before the war of 1967, *The Thief of Bagdad*. Every time I passed the cinema, I felt time had stopped and our life was spent waiting for the old film to be changed.

It had not been a good time for Esther. Her husband's health was deteriorating. She stayed indoors nursing him most of the day, deprived of the distraction of afternoon movie-going. But she had a cinematic adventure that occupied her mind as she sat on the porch of her house: how to retrieve the jewellery she had left in Jaffa.

In 1948 all her acquaintances and friends had thought that they would be leaving their homes for no more than a few weeks, until the Jewish terror from the Stern Gang ended. But Esther had thought otherwise. Before they left she had gone to her garden, dug a hole and buried the metal box in which she kept her jewellery. After the 1967 war she went to the priest in the Orthodox church and prevailed upon him to go to her house in Jaffa. She described the location where she had dug the hole, between the two lemon trees and five metres away from the gate. The priest could not refuse Esther's wish and did as she commanded. He found the house, but more trees had grown in the garden. He stood by the gate observing the house and trying not to attract attention, waiting for the occupants to leave and wondering where he should dig. It was a scene reminiscent of the treasure hunt in the film *It's a Mad Mad Mad Mad World*. And as the hero in that film suddenly figured out the site where the treasure was buried between the palm trees forming a large 'W', so the priest identified the place where Esther had buried her treasure. When he came back to Ramallah and knocked on Esther's door he was carrying with him the rusty metal box full of Esther's precious jewellery.

A few years after this incident I went to visit Esther to ask after her husband. It was not the best time to visit. Mr Jallad, for whom I had great respect, was dying. Esther was in the room with him. The door was closed and the other members of her family were standing in the lobby, waiting for Esther to emerge. When she finally did, she walked towards us and, after closing the door behind her, announced in French, '*C'est fini.*' Her face bore that same solemn expression she had when on her way to the cinema. Her lips were pursed, but her beautiful black eyes were not smudged with pink eyeshadow; they were red from the tears she had silently shed in that darkened room as her husband breathed his last. I was saddened by the loss of the venerable old man but could not help marvelling at how unreal it felt. Esther's dramatic words sounded like a line adapted from one of the movies she had watched at Cinema Dunia.

Mr Jallad's death marked the end of an era, the demise of that class of well-to-do refugees from Jaffa who, in spite of having lost everything, kept their dignity and pursued their lives in their new homes as best they could manage, often resorting to the movies for escape from the dismal, desperate reality around them. Most had left after the occupation to start new lives yet again in prosperous Amman. Now the last of those who remained had died.

Without a husband to nurse, all her children abroad and no cinema to escape to, Esther moved to Amman to live with her daughter. Her unmarried granddaughter was kind to her. When Esther could no longer leave the house to visit the cinema, she gave her a video player so she could dim the lights in her room and view, alone, lying in bed, her favourite movies. To her amazement, Esther never used it. It was not for the films that Esther would go to the cinema: rather it was being in the dark, watching films with others, young and old, who came for all sorts of reasons, and then leaving the emotionally charged, smoky hall for the other world outside, having made that other world seem different.

Meanwhile, in Ramallah, complaints about the dullness of life in the Palestinian towns were mounting. Bethlehem was the first to reopen its movie houses, closed since June 1967. Jerusalem followed and finally Ramallah. By the end of the year all the movie houses that had been in operation before the war resumed their activities. Without access to the Arab world, the only films that could be screened were those which the cinemas already had in store or which came via Israel. This meant fewer Arabic films. *Ajnabi* films were brought from Israel. Instead of Arabic subtitles, these films were subtitled in Hebrew, which no one could read.

With such poor fare, the audience, which came enthusiastically at first, starved as it was of any sort of film, soon began to dwindle. The censor was gone and the national anthem a quirk of the past. And with most of the audience only able to look at the pictures and hardly understand a third of what was being said because of poor English and no knowledge of written Hebrew, what mattered was the sensation of seeing these actors perform all sorts of exciting scenes on the big screen. It was not long before the cinemas went a step further and began to show films that depended entirely on the visual without the need to follow a narrative line: that is, pornography.

These proved to be very popular. Once again movie houses began to fill up, but now with an exclusively male audience. And without censorship or control, there was nothing to deter young teenagers, eager to smoke out of sight of their parents, from coming to sit in the movie house, watching one pornographic film after another and puffing away.

While Cinema Dunia in Ramallah showed pornographic films only occasionally, Al Nuzha Cinema in Jerusalem seemed to specialise in the genre. Complaints began. Teachers were concerned about the effect on their students. Parents also made their voices heard. Then the notorious Nuzha burned down. It remained derelict until it was taken over by a group of dramatists, who established the first Palestinian theatre, the Hakawati, later also to be turned into the first cinema club in East Jerusalem.

Cinema Dunia was not burned but bowed to self-censorship and only occasionally slipped in a pornographic movie. It was eventually Israeli taxes that forced it out of business in 1984. The other two movie houses in Ramallah continued until the First Intifada erupted at the end of 1987. Then, a few years later, they too were forced to close down when the Israeli army began storming the darkened theatre to arrest suspected activists who were taking time off from resistance.

All the cinemas remained closed until the Oslo Accords brought a measure of false hope and Cinema Walid reopened. It still had that same smell of disinfectant in the toilets. But Cinema Dunia had closed down for good. Cinema Jameel was renamed as the Kasaba Ciné-Club and turned into a theatre hosting plays and showed a combination of popular movies and films of quality.

In Amman, Esther was in her ninth decade. One day she called her granddaughter into her room and told her to go to the wardrobe and pull out the lacy dress she had brought with her from Jaffa when they left in 1948 and had not since had an occasion to wear. The granddaughter asked if she wished to wear it. 'No, my dear,' said Esther. 'It is not for now. It is for later. You know what I mean.'

The granddaughter's eyes filled with tears. 'No, *Tata*! No, no!'

'Yes, my dear. I want you to promise to put this on me when the end comes.'

Not long after, the time came for Esther to escape into the final dark hall that awaits us all. She went in style, dressed in her best gown, as elegant as she always had been when she walked down from her house for shorter escapes into Cinema Dunia.

20 JULY

For days I have been checking the mail and finding the box empty. Finally yesterday there was one *New York Review of Books* and one *London Review of Books* (we have missed many more), but there was also a letter in Penny's mailbox from a man, a good man, in Israel who said that he received a book from Blackwell's along with another that the mail had sent to him though it was destined for Penny and had her address. This was why he was writing to her, asking where he should send it. Is the Israeli post office directing our mail of books and parcels to Israelis? Anything is possible.

21 JULY

Only after seeing the new city of Rawabi being constructed in the hills north of Ramallah did I understand the full ramifications of our defeat. Rather than struggle to gain our own space and assert our own way of life, we seek to copy the coloniser and use the same destructive methods that damage our land and natural heritage.

Today I took part in what was billed as an Urban Bus Tour, sponsored by what was called the Designing Civic Encounter Initiative. Architects from Ramallah's Riwaq Center would be our guides and explain what the Oslo years have done to urban planning.

We started at the highest spot in Ramallah, the site of the old Muqata'a, where the Tegart Building used to be. This is a fortress made of reinforced concrete built just after the Arab Revolt of 1936 against the British Mandate. It is one of some fifty such structures built in various parts of Palestine, initiated by Sir Charles Tegart, a former Commissioner of Police in Calcutta. He was sent to Palestine as a counterterrorism expert in the midst of the 1936 Revolt. He had other inspirational ideas which were adopted by the Mandate officials, including building a security wall along the northern border of Palestine to prevent infiltration, importing Dobermann pinschers from South Africa and establishing a special centre in Jerusalem to train

The crowded Jalazone Refugee Camp, north of Ramallah, where
13,000 Palestinians are living on 253 *dunums* of land.

interrogators in torture techniques. The Arafat Mausoleum, museum and mosque now stand on the site of the fortress.

No competition was held to choose the most suitable design for this public place so fraught with meaning and imbued with history. A Palestinian architect from Amman, talented but with no direct experience of the residents' suffering under occupation, was appointed the Palestinian Authority's court architect. He did not ask what we wished to see there. His sponsor in the Authority arranged for Israel to grant him a permit to visit. He came, looked around, went back to his office in Amman and came up with the design. I felt so cheated, so hurt. It is true that most of the structure had been bombed by the Israelis when Arafat was hiding there during the 2002 invasion. Some parts could have been restored. And even if this were not possible, at least some consideration should have been given to what the place meant to the Palestinian public, not just the one man who was responsible for landing us with the worst surrender document in our history, the Oslo Accords.

We then proceeded to see some of the effects of Oslo in the village of Bir Nabala, north of Jerusalem. This had always been a kind of suburb of Jerusalem but has now been cut off by the wall. Our guide called it a case of urban amputation. It has plenty of empty apartments abandoned by holders of Jerusalem residency cards who can no longer live there. Before the wall isolated it, the village used to be reached via the main Ramallah–Jerusalem road. It is now accessed from Ramallah through a tunnel running beneath the highway connecting the settlements of Givat Zeev and others with Jerusalem. But this is closed to Arab residents. Being in Area C, only Israeli authorities can issue building permits there. So unlike Ramallah, which is overcrowded, Bir Nabala has plenty of empty space – into which Ramallah cannot expand.

Yet rather than fight the battle to lift the restrictions on building in the confined villages spread throughout the West Bank, a group of local and Qatari investors set their sights on one of the most attractive hills north of Ramallah which rises 780 metres above sea level. Two and a half years ago they began buying terraced land cultivated with olives, from unsuspecting farmers for knock-down prices, in order to build the new city of Rawabi. They needed 6,300 *dunams* to accommodate 25,000 residents. The land they were unable to buy had to be confiscated by the Palestinian Authority.

Our group sat on benches at long tables made from tree trunks under a shaded area overlooking the hills being destroyed by bulldozers below, with waves of dirt and dust from the excavated land sweeping over us. The scene was reminiscent of how American Jews are brought to Israel, to admire what the settlers are building in the land of the Bible. The young man was doing his best to paint a rosy picture of the project. He explained how they had made an environmental impact study and how the trees they had had to uproot had been replanted just above where we were sitting, waiting to be uprooted again once the building was done. I turned to where he pointed and saw a little cluster of forlorn-looking trees struggling to survive, covered in dust.

Can Qatar be blamed? It succeeded in building booming cities in the desert, so why not in the empty hills of the West Bank? This is not a desert. Qataris don't know the terrain. Most of them have never visited.

'Our vision,' said the young manager, 'is to get the economy for peace going by creating jobs, increasing capacity building, creating sustainable design without pollution.' He kept repeating, 'The environment is of prime concern to us.' How could he expect to convince anyone when we could see the attractive village of Ajoul close by and contrast it with the sterile monstrosity that was being erected on hills destroyed for that purpose? To get to this artificial creation more roads will be needed. All this to house 25,000 middle-class Palestinians who could easily have found homes in the villages surrounding Ramallah had an effort been exerted by the Authority to pressure the Israelis to loosen their control over land-use planning. The unchallenged Israeli plan is to confine the spatial expansion of these villages in order to leave the land empty for the future 'natural growth' of their own settlements.

One of the urban planners made the point that, despite everything that had been said, in his experience planned cities never worked. How sad that we Palestinians are destroying the landscape around us just as the Israelis have long been doing. We seem to be competing with them over who can create the greatest damage in the shortest period of time.

On the way we crossed over from Ramallah through the hills using the bypass road illegally built by the settlers on private land right after the Oslo deal was signed. I had never driven on this road before. It is no longer used by the settlers and so is now open to Palestinians. I wish I hadn't. I looked out at the few remaining pockets of unspoiled nature in the valley where I had enjoyed so many good walks. The hills are now cluttered with piles of rubble from new construction work and roads being built as Ramallah expands. Our guide pointed out two housing projects that looked exactly like Jewish settlements, with rows of identical houses one next to the other, totally alien to our traditional way of building. One of these projects is on valuable public land that our late president, Arafat, simply gave away to those who had served as diplomats in return for their imperceptible contributions to our cause. The other project was the work of the Palestine Investment Fund, which also confuses the private and the public. At public expense, they make available services that benefit only a select few. Palestine is being sold off piecemeal, with an unprecedented frenzy of land-destroying construction of buildings and roads.

Our trip ended at the Jalazone Refugee Camp north of Ramallah. Perhaps the tour organisers wanted us to see the disparity between Rawabi, where 25,000 Palestinians will be housed on 6,800 *dunams*, and Jalazone, where about half this number, 13,000, are living on only 253 *dunams*.

I came back home exhausted, sad, with dusty shoes, a blocked nose and clouded thoughts.

22 JULY

This news item appeared in last week's *Ha'aretz*:

> *More than 60,000 Palestinians expected to visit Israel in 2011 – as tourists from the West Bank*

> Civil administration sources said: 'We want Palestinians especially young ones to see another kind of Israeli, not only soldiers and settlers. Anything that can help them blow off steam and relax. Perhaps instead of demonstrating in September they'll go to the beach.'
> The guide said: 'In addition to ecologic [*sic*] explanations we try to convey a message of coexistence between animals and human beings, and among people as well. Politics does not come into it. It's a completely different atmosphere and they're engrossed in looking at the animals ... for many of these youngsters this is the first

The Israeli army often uses the most arable land as firing zones.

visit to the beach, they see things differently from Israeli children. They've never seen wild animals like those in the safari.'

Penny was appalled to see Palestinians described as tourists. I didn't feel the same. Since Oslo I have felt myself a tourist in Israel, much as I try to resist this and convince myself that it is otherwise.

23 JULY

So, after an Arab Spring, now perhaps a Palestinian Summer? It is no secret that the First Intifada was possible because there were no loans, no mortgages, nothing to fear because there was not much to lose.

Then, after Oslo, everything was done to encourage the banks to grow and arrange loans until we became walking loans. And the law changed, making it possible to own a flat, when earlier it was possible to own only an unspecified share in a building.

The new course of economic development was determined by a political agenda inspired by Western funders and supported by the Palestinian Authority for ending the resistance before we had liberated our land and won our freedom. From potential revolutionaries we are turned into hostages to banks established since the Oslo deal.

So much for a revolutionary uprising.

Most of our greengrocers come from the Hebron region in the south of the West Bank. This morning once again I saw that many of our vegetables and most of our fruit now come from Israel. Since last year's olive harvest over 9,000 trees, primarily olive trees, have been damaged or destroyed by settlers. So much land has been taken from Palestinian farmers, who were also deprived of water, that we now have to rely on Israel for most of our food. The Palestinian Authority does not help the farmers – it taxes them while the price of fuel is so high that transporting the produce from the farm to the market is prohibitively expensive. Whereas the budget for security is 35 per cent, agriculture gets a mere 2 per cent.

When I used to pass through the Faraa Valley, which runs parallel to the Jordan Valley to the east, I used to find it lush and green, but now I see many of the fields lying fallow. A sign on one of them declares the land an Israeli army firing zone, evidence of the role the army plays in the process of land acquisition for settlements. By the road is a sign for 'Organica', where the settlers grow organic food, and another for a fish farm. It is devastating to think of the suffering of farmers whose land is taken away so that they end up having to work as labourers for others, cultivating land they used to own, or to clean fish ponds when they have no water for their crops.

The Israeli belief that they are entitled by divine right to this land and its riches, whether buried in the ground or falling from the sky, extends to preventing farmers from placing water catchment pools above their land to collect rainwater for irrigation. They simply refuse to grant the required licence. Presumably this is because the rainwater descending from the heavens should not be prevented from replenishing underground reservoirs which are under exclusive Israeli control.

We can still buy eggs from Palestinian farmers. In Israel, since the state was formed, milk and egg production have been considered 'Zionist agricultural branches' that could be practised only by Jewish agricultural settlements.

Palestinian farmers have been excluded from the production of milk and eggs; their sale in Israel requires a licence from the Agricultural Ministry and this has been denied them.

24 JULY

Ramallah and its sister city, Bireh, are surrounded to the east and north by two Jewish settlements, Psagot and Beit Eil. The first is secular, the second Orthodox. Now Psagot is producing wines, about which I've just been reading. They are kept in a nearby cave in the hills which only the settlers can now enjoy and use. The wine is Cabernet Sauvignon, one of my favourites. The romanticism of the whole process is alluring: wine from vineyards near Ramallah left to ferment in an ancient cave. Strongly reminiscent of the vineyards that used to cover the hills around the city where I live. And the price was not exorbitant for the stock. If I need wine, why not buy it from there, only a five minutes' drive away? The only problem is that it is made in an illegal settlement.

25 JULY

This month marks seven years since the International Court of Justice ruled that the wall is illegal and should be torn down. Yet it continues to be built, keeping children away from their schools and farmers from their fields, and tearing families apart.

Another monster of a 'fence' is being built along Israel's border with Egypt. The country is adamant on walling itself in on all sides.

1 AUGUST

Remembering Mother and her suffering on the second anniversary of her death has made me more keenly aware than ever before of the passage of time, the cycle of generations and how I too am part of it all.

Father and Mother belonged to the generation of the Nakba. They lived the experience and suffered it their entire lives. I belong to the generation of the 1967 defeat, which we call the Nakseh. The present generation is that of Oslo, with its heavy toll of defeat disguised as victory and its measure of false glamour.

2 AUGUST

The Orthodox Jews in the old city have taken to spitting on the Christian orthodox prelates, whether Greek Orthodox or Armenian. Anyone in Christian robes.

One young priest hit back and was pardoned by the Israeli court.

7 AUGUST

Protests over house prices that began in Israel two weeks ago are gathering steam. Even Israel, it seems, is having an Arab Spring.

So much for Netanyahu's words in Washington, describing Israel to the US Congress as the one country that has 'no tremors, no protests, that is stable, this Israeli democracy where everyone is equal under the law'.

And yet it is strange for me to be following the housing crisis in Israel with such enthusiasm, hoping it will become the beginning of a serious protest movement against the government. This is the protest of Jewish Israelis who want cheaper housing and cheaper cottage cheese. They are protesting for equality for themselves alone. They are the members of the group to whom the whole land has been assigned, who discriminate against the original owners of the land and do not recognise their rights to the land, nor fully recognise the rights of the Israeli citizens of non-Jewish extraction. They are only protesting for themselves. That is all. Nothing to do with me or my people. So why am I hopeful?

The country, which began with socialist ideals I found attractive, nevertheless always discriminated against the non-Jew. The communal kibbutz movement had no qualms about espousing principles of equality and social justice to practise on land that had been confiscated from Palestinians forcibly ejected from it.

Still there were things to admire about Israel. The sense of solidarity and the ability to organise a state that began to function well within a short period of time. When socialist dreams ceased to motivate large numbers of Jews to come to settle the land, offers of subsidised homes became the incentive. When I began to read about the ways of this country of which I had known nothing until it occupied the West Bank, I felt conflicted. I read about the Tolstoyan ideals espoused by some of the early settlers and realized they were values that I entirely supported; yet they were ultimately used as a means for the exact opposite objective, to colonise the place and replace one group with another.

In time things changed, both physically and practically. Now the colonisation process has spread to the West Bank, where settlements like Ariel have been established on land taken from Palestinians. No longer does the country market itself as a socialist Utopia but rather as a comfortable middle-class paradise where families can have the space they need, fresh air, wonderful views, swimming pools, for the most part all free of any trace of a Palestinian presence.

9 AUGUST

What I have been dreading has happened. A joint group of forty-two cabinet ministers and members of the Israeli Knesset (all of them members of the Eretz Israel lobby) signed a petition addressed to the prime minister, calling on him to solve the housing crisis that has swept the country – by building in the West Bank and Jerusalem. There was a 500 per cent increase in settlement housing start-ups in the first half of 2011. Settlers are calling on Netanyahu to expedite construction of 4,500 units across the West Bank. 'The only obstacle preventing this construction,' declares a political advertisement addressed to the prime minister, 'is your signature and that of the defence minister. If you will only sign, we can solve the housing problems of 4,500 families.'

It is an odd situation but its internal contradictions have not yet come to the fore and been exploited. Here is a government that offers incentives to one group, the settlers, and provides housing for them at subsidised rates, but which is unwilling to provide adequate housing for those who do not wish to live as colonisers in West Bank settlements. And yet the protesters have not raised this political anomaly. They call on the government to fulfil their demands without asking it to cease its illegal policies of settlement. They want to have it both ways.

11 AUGUST

I was way off the mark when I asked last year at the Khan Theatre why the Israelis do not learn to speak Arabic. I have just learned that lawmakers from both the governing coalition and the opposition in Israel have submitted a proposal to the Knesset for a new Basic Law to replace the definition of Israel as 'a Jewish and democratic state' with the state as the 'national home for the Jewish people'. They also propose removing Arabic, the language spoken by no fewer than a quarter of the population, as one of the official languages of the state. This would mean there was no obligation to mark street and road signs in Arabic as well as Hebrew and English, and would no doubt save many the 'humiliation' of having to see Arabic lettering in public spaces. Then they can live in total denial that they exist in a region inhabited by millions of Arabs.

12 AUGUST

In the understatement of the year Shimon Peres, Israel's president, the man who must have been instrumental in getting the largest number of illegal Jewish settlements built on occupied Palestinian land, told a visiting delegation of US congressmen that 'peace is encountering difficulties'. Yet he still believes it is achievable, 'as always'.

13 AUGUST

Exactly fifty years have passed since the East German government built a wall which was euphemistically described as 'an anti-fascist protection measure'. A minute's silence was observed across Germany at noon. When will we observe our minute of silence?

11 SEPTEMBER

Yesterday Penny and I went to soak in the sulphur baths at the Dead Sea. On the way I thought more of the idea that the Israeli people are like any other, some good and some bad, but it is their political system which encourages wickedness. Their politicians survive by being more right wing and extreme; there is no reward for moderation or for a longer-term vision. At present, the scariest manifestation of this is the beating of the drums of war against Iran. Netanyahu finds himself in a bind over the negotiations with the Palestinians and needs a distraction. If the war is waged we will surely be in great danger. The only consolation is, as one columnist has commented, that if they really intended to wage war they would not be speaking so much about it. They might be using it as a threat to win greater sanctions against Iran.

12 SEPTEMBER

My car battery died today. After jump-starting the car I took it to the garage and hired a taxi to get home. On the way back the driver said that tears came to his eyes this morning when he heard the mother of one of the long-term prisoners on the radio saying that when she visits her son in jail and speaks about new technology he doesn't know what she's referring to. The driver said, 'These long-term prisoners might think Facebook is a kind of food. So many of the electronic gadgets we use, including mobile phones, became popular only in the last ten years. Some who were arrested as young men have aged in jail, with no sign that they will ever be released.' Then we spoke about the new measures by the Israeli Prison Authorities against the prisoners, including placing many in solitary confinement, denying them the right to pursue university education, limiting prison visits, allowing only one hour per day of exercise and handcuffing them when they meet with their lawyers. It was unbearable.

To dinner at one of the newly opened restaurants in Ramallah. As we sat in the congenial surroundings I thought how unlikely it looks that any public protests might start any time soon. But just before the First Intifada I remember thinking exactly this. Then in a matter of days everything changed. Perhaps the prisoners will be unable to take the new regime and will go on strike. This might spark public protests and a new Intifada would begin. Everything is possible in our volatile region.

13 SEPTEMBER

What a relief it is to be ending the decade dominated by the terrible attack on New York by the Bin Laden supporters. Those who destroyed the twin towers, like those who lynched the Israelis in Ramallah in 2002, are criminals, murderers of the worst kind. These are not acts of war. However, attributing what is purely the criminal action of a few to an entire religion, while calling a legitimate struggle criminal, serves only to confuse the issues, corrupts language and minds, fuels intolerance and discrimination, and can easily lead to more of those same horrors that such blind reactions mean to condemn. Israel is also guilty of contributing substantially to the corruption of political language. Since the 1970s it has been calling all those who resist occupation 'terrorists'. The beneficiaries of real and imagined terrorism are Israel's business moguls. Israeli security firms now have about 4 per cent of the global business of designing, manufacturing and selling security devices and systems.

14 SEPTEMBER

On the radio in the shared taxi I took to work this morning I heard a recording of Arafat's declaration of a Palestinian state on 15 November 1988. Three days later, Penny and I were married, so the date is imprinted on my mind. The psychological impact of the words that the Palestinians declared 'the establishment of the state of Palestine on our Palestinian territory with its capital Jerusalem' were tremendous. For many decades Israel has been doing all it can to deny the very existence of Palestine and the Palestinians.

People I speak to about Palestine's UN bid for recognition as a state are generally sceptical. They think it is just a distraction, a gimmick. They realize that much of the land has been taken by Israel and that no UN resolution will change this. An architect in his late fifties with whom I spoke said the important thing is that 'we have managed to resist the Israeli attempts at driving us away from the land. Even the buildings we construct are solid. We use stone, not flimsy material that can be easily swept away by a storm. We are here to stay. We've proved ourselves by our resilience. If the harsh forty-four years of occupation have not managed to make us budge, nothing will.'

Perhaps sometimes the tables are turned. Last week about forty Israeli passengers on a Turkish Airlines flight from Tel Aviv to Istanbul had their passports taken away and were then detained for several hours by Turkish police for questioning. Their bags were opened and searched, and they were asked the reason for their visit to Turkey, how much money they were carrying and what they had on their laptops. Authorities in Israel believe that the detention of the Israeli passengers came in response to a recent incident when Turkish citizens were subjected to similar treatment by border police at Ben-Gurion Airport.

After all these years of Palestinian suffering and humiliation at Israeli ports of entry, no Arab country allowing Israelis to enter has ever dared to treat them in a similar manner. Until the Istanbul incident, Israelis were never given any hint that they might one day have to pay for their mistreatment of Palestinian Arabs and Muslims from neighbouring countries.

In the evening Penny and I were sitting on the roof having a drink and watching the sun set. We remembered how we used to walk around the foundations of our house, wondering when it would be completed. We have now enjoyed fourteen years in this house. From our roof, with the tops of the trees in our garden and the olive grove behind us, Ramallah looks less obnoxious. Most of the hills around that used to be empty when we first moved in are already scarred with buildings, and in the distance we can see many more settlements dominating the tops of the surrounding hills.

When the sun begins to set the speed of the wind increases, as if waving farewell to the sun. Eventually it calms down. Then the crescent moon rises. We still have one small corner free of high-rise buildings through which we can see all the way to the Mediterranean coast. As darkness falls lights begin to sparkle. On clear evenings like this the view is spectacular.

15 SEPTEMBER

Last night Penny and I had dinner with a dear Israeli friend now in her eighties. Judy Blanc and I had participated in a speaking tour in the early 1980s to try and mobilise European public opinion on the issues of the day: then as now, settlements and the occupation. Judy has never stopped being an activist, still going to demonstrations and thinking about what can be done. While she sides with the young activists who protest against the wall and are involved in the struggle against the settlers in Sheikh Jarrah, her view of the Tel Aviv protests was much dimmer. Judy, always seeing for herself, went to talk to the protesters and came away convinced that they were not moving beyond their own material interests, which were mainly middle-class and definitely not shared with either their fellow Palestinian citizens or those beyond the Green Line under occupation.

16 SEPTEMBER

It is said that the huge public protest in Israel started over an increase in the price of cottage cheese made by the Israeli company Tnuva. I have now sampled the brand in question and found it to be disappointing, lacking in flavour, barely reminiscent of the real thing. But it led me to think that there is a lesson here on how and when to expect the Israeli public to rise up in protest. What if the continuation of the occupation began to hurt rather than benefit the average Israeli economically, as it has been doing so far? If the price of cottage cheese caused such a stir, how much more could happen if the occupation begins to exact a cost on Israel?

Prompted by the forthcoming Palestinian bid for statehood at the UN, I have been asked by a number of media outlets whether I think a Palestinian state in the Occupied Territories is still feasible. Listening to the way the journalists pose the question has made me aware of how we are locked in the present. The assumption is that the day after the peace all will remain as it is now, with the check-points and closed borders staying in place, the hatred and the anger. People cannot extend their minds to the future and think beyond the present parameters.

In 1979 Menachem Begin said he wanted to create a political reality whereby no Israeli government could give up 'Judea and Samaria' (the biblical names of the West Bank). He seems to have succeeded, but only because the right wing are winning the psychological war which posits the argument that the settlements can never be evacuated.

If France could move one million French citizens out of Algeria why can't Israel move 450,000 (many of whom have second homes in the settlements)? Of course they would if they had to or if they felt it was necessary for the survival of the country.

17 SEPTEMBER

The skewed sense of justice the settlers exhibit results in making both Palestinians and Israeli Jews who do not support them pay a price for actions taken by the army to enforce the law in the West Bank and remove what in Israel's own eyes are illegal settlements. They call this the 'price tag' policy. For every action taken by the army, the settlers will exact a price by killing Palestinians, destroying their property and in some cases directing their violence against fellow Israelis. Today, settlers attacked twelve Israeli military vehicles after the army began removing mobile homes from the outpost of Migron. The home of a well-known Israeli left-wing activist in Jerusalem was defaced with graffiti proclaiming 'death to the traitors' and 'price tag Migron'. Rare moments when we Palestinians and the Israeli army and people are in the same boat.

18 SEPTEMBER

Just back from the annual Muwatin Conference. For many years now the conference has had to do with our own small world of Palestine, but things have changed. This one is concerned with the effect on Palestine of the Arab Spring and the effect on the Arab states of the Palestinian cause. So our horizons are widening, together with our links to the rest of the Arab world.

One of the speakers said that the conditions that allow people to be reborn only come about every hundred years or so – a rare opportunity that must be seized. What is taking place in the Arab world is a series of revolutions that were neither instigated nor led by a party or traditional political leaders. In the past there were many coups but never revolutions. He also pointed out that change in the Arab world had been made hostage to the Palestinian state and Palestine's liberation. The Palestine–Israel conflict was used as a barrier in the face of change. What has happened has liberated the Arabs from this bondage. It had always been said: first Palestine, then change in the Arab regimes. The revolutions changed this.

Last night Abbas made a speech in which he confirmed that the PLO will be taking the request for Palestinian statehood first to the General Assembly and then to the Security Council. Our president has the air of a headmaster. True to this image, he described how in the past two years no effort has been spared to develop Palestine and turn it into a well-run entity. We've done our homework! Abbas then said that if people demonstrated they should not use violence, so as to deny Israel any excuse to use violence against us. That is, he exhorted us to remain good, well-behaved boys and girls and not upset the teacher. In other words, he was saying that we've all been well behaved, we've worked hard, passed all the exams and followed all the rules. Now we deserve a good grade and report card, which the principal, Ban Ki-Moon, will hand over. If only there was that sort of justice in the world.

Billboards are sprouting up all over town, advertising Palestine's bid for statehood at the UN. They are written in both Arabic and English. Those in Irsal Street near the Muqata'a announce in bad English: 'Statehood is our right, Freedom is our desting.' If the local public is the audience for these, why bother to use English at all? Especially misspelt English? Another reads: 'It is time for Palestine UN 194.'

Palestine would be country number 194 to join the UN. Few are aware that this is also the number of the General Assembly resolution of 11 December 1948, stating that 'the refugees wishing to return to their homes and live at peace with their neighbours should be permitted to do so at the earliest practicable date, and that compensation should be paid for the property of those choosing not to return ...' Of course, it is just another of the many UN resolutions that have never been implemented.

We are told that the actual replica of a UN General Assembly seat that Palestine has sent to roam the world is getting closer to New York. We should be cheering!

19 SEPTEMBER

I was at the office when I received a call from Adli Dirhali in Amman and we started chatting about Jaffa as though it were a place we both knew and had left only last week. Born in 1936, he still remembers everything about Jaffa. The reason he called was that he had recently read my book *Strangers in the House*. 'Will there be a new edition soon?' he asked. I wanted to know why he was interested. He explained that I need to remove the reference to Cinema Rivoli, because no cinema of that name had existed in Jaffa. The Jaffa cinemas were Al Hambra, El Farouk El Rashid, Nabeel, El Shark (which showed action films) and Al Touki (which was the very first cinema to open there). The Apollo had been demolished.

He then told me about Kahwat Abu Shakoush, which was the VIPs' café. It called itself a stage and a café, *masrah wa kahwa*, where famous singers like Um Kalthoum performed. It was in this café, he said, that my father used to sit. Kahwat el Tuyus, on the other hand, was the café of the idle and those who made money by leasing their orange groves and had nothing to do for the rest of the year.

I asked him if he knew the address of Father's law office in Jaffa. He had the information ready at hand. 'It was either at Iskandar Awad Street or Bistriss Street, which were in fact two sections of the same street.'

When I put the phone down I thought of what Simon Goldhill has written about the Jewish Temple after its destruction by the Titus in AD 70:

> The Tractate Middoth, 'Measurements', ... rehearses the measurements of Herod's Temple, cubit by cubit, and runs through the map of the building, recording the use of different rooms ... The map is not merely laid out for us: it is staged as a threat of forgetting defeated by an act of memory. To study is to memorialise the destroyed Temple.

Has Jaffa become a monument of the imagination for displaced Palestinians as the destroyed Temple is for religious Jews?

Going through Father's papers after Mother died, I saw a letter from the man Father appointed to take care of his house during their absence in 1948. He must not have realized he would never be able to get it back.

Just as the present residents of Jaffa are worried about the creeping Jewish settlement of the Orthodox Jews in their midst, so are the secular residents of Haifa. Two weeks ago they learned from a newspaper advertisement that the municipality planned to allot a neighbourhood shelter to a Haredi [ultra Orthodox] organisation for use as a community centre. An ultra-Orthodox nursery school is also in the works for the street, near two secular nurseries.

Professor Yossi Ben Artzi of the University of Haifa, who lives in the neighbourhood, says the municipality's actions 'will cause veteran neighbourhood residents to flee from Neveh Sha'anan. This is a process to turn Neveh Sha'anan into the ultra-Orthodox town of Bnei Brak. I'm not saying they don't deserve a place to live. There are abandoned neighbourhoods in Haifa – the entire lower area of Hadar and even Wadi Salib.'

This was the area where the family of my maternal grandmother lived until 1948, when they were forced out. But there is no suggestion that these 'abandoned' areas will be returned to their Palestinian owners, even though the secularists do not want them to go to the Orthodox.

20 SEPTEMBER

There are now almost daily incidents of killings, burning and cutting of olive and fig trees, expropriations of land and calls by right-wing factions in the government to annex the settlements. This morning settlers from the settlement of Ravava, armed with power saws, destroyed 500 olive and fig trees in Wadi Abu Dras, west of the village of Karawa Beni Hussan. Then there was a case of arson in the olive orchards of the city of Qalqilya in the north of the West Bank which lie on land the wall has put on the Israeli side. Most likely the fire was started by arsonists from the settlement of Tzofim. Palestinian firefighters were not allowed to put it out.

The settlers are also trying to enter Palestinian villages and intimidate the inhabitants. In the villages of Assera and Oreef they shot two boys, aged fourteen and eighteen. A Palestinian organisation calling itself 'We Refuse to Die Silently' has been documenting these events and reports that a force of forty settlers protected by the Israeli army tried to enter the two villages but were stopped by the villagers. One house was firebombed. Settlers have also tried to enter the village of Yabid. They set fire to 400 trees in Jenin and ninety *dunams* of the lands of Qalqilya.

The settlers and their lobby say, 'Well, this is our land and so nothing that we do to keep it is unjustified. We should go all the way.' If this were a play on a grand scale, then we are reaching the denouement. And the audience, which is the rest of the world, will be forced to weigh in on one side or the other and either applaud or decry the victory of one of the two contestants.

According to an internal Israeli government document that has been leaked, Israeli troops distributed maps with red lines drawn on them around Israeli settlements in the West Bank, with instructions to soldiers that if Palestinian protesters got too close to the settlements, they should be shot in the legs.

The instructions do not differentiate between non-violent demonstrations and violent attacks, thus implying that non-violent demonstrators would be shot in the legs if they crossed a 'line' whose location had never been shared with Palestinians.

Security guards hired by Israeli settlements in the West Bank have attended training sessions held by the Israeli military where they learned methods of subduing protests using both non-lethal and lethal violence. Engaging with Palestinian protesters outside settlement boundaries is beyond the purview of settlement security guards, but the Israeli military has authorised the guards to act as a branch of the military during future protests.

The leaked document also includes a statement by the Israeli military that they are making extensive preparations 'to deal with incidents near the fences and the borders of the state of Israel'. Although the state of Israel has never defined its borders since its creation in 1948, the reference to 'borders' appears to refer to the edges of Israeli settlements.

This latest operation has been dubbed 'Operation Summer Seeds', which sounds ominously similar to the 2006 operation over Gaza, 'Operation Summer Rains', when Israel dropped 40,000 sound grenades and live missiles on the Strip over the course of the summer. During the past decade we've had no fewer than six major operations. We had the 2002 invasion of West Bank cities which was called 'Operation Defensive Shield'. It was followed in May 2004 by 'Operation Rainbow' and 'Operation Days of Penitence' in October 2004. After the 2006 'Operation Summer Rains' against Gaza, there was 'Operation Hot Winter' in 2008, also against Gaza, followed by the massive assault of 2009 dubbed 'Operation Cast Lead'. Then for a change of atmosphere, the operation against the flotilla in the Mediterranean was called 'Operation Sea Breeze'.

One analyst who studied the names given to Israeli

military operations between 1948 and 2007 found that
more than 60 per cent of them alluded to either the natural
world or the Bible, metaphorical names intended to suggest
that the campaigns were either forces of nature or sanc-
tioned by a higher power. 'The basic theoretical supposition
is that military naming is a simple and useful mechanism
that might be employed to blur undesired aspects – such
as the human and economical costs – associated with
the respective practices,' writes Dalia Gavriely-Nuri of
Hadassah College, Jerusalem, and Bar-Ilan University, the
researcher who conducted the study. 'Operation First Rain'
and 'Operation Lightning Strike' suggest these operations
are an 'inevitable, natural event, rather than one worthy of
public examination'.

Meanwhile, in the settlement of Kiryat Arba in the
Hebron area in the south, inaugural celebrations are taking
place at the new cultural centre (perhaps to compete with
that of Ariel in the north), including speeches by several
high-profile politicians. The centre is being boycotted by
many artists in Israel. One member of the Kiryat Arba
council said that the organisers would not 'grovel before any
traitor from the state of Tel Aviv' who refuses to perform
here. So wide has the gap grown that Tel Aviv is considered
a separate state.

21 SEPTEMBER

Took a walk along Ramallah's Main Street. The pavements
have been widened and new attractive lanterns put along
them. Pedestrians are kept away from the road itself by
chains. Now I am used to them, but when I first saw them
I was shocked. Yet despite these efforts by the municipality to keep the street free from jaywalkers, people still

pass through the moving cars, which makes driving nerve-racking. Some of the shops I recognise from when I was a child, like Rukab's ice cream parlour. But they have all been renovated and smartened up. The only building that has remained as I remember it is the Friends' Meeting House of the Quakers.

The other change is the way the traffic now speeds along. In the past cars used to crawl through Ramallah streets. Now they zoom. There are many reasons for this. The streets are no longer potholed. New straight, wide streets have been opened and traffic lights have been installed. When the city was under direct Israeli occupation we were not allowed, obviously for security reasons, to have traffic lights. For army jeeps and the settler cars to have to stop was deemed a security risk. The zooming cars also reflect greater confidence in the order of things; that there are rules which are likely to be observed by others means you can speed along.

Just as you can read a lot about the character of a person from the way they drive, so can you read the state of a society from the way its traffic is organised and how its drivers behave. The Israelis act as if they're driving a tank, taking risks without seeming to be aware of the presence of others on the road. More have died in traffic accidents than in the many wars they have fought.

When I got to the Manarah Circle in the centre of town I saw 'The Chair'. And what a chair! Gigantic with huge legs, imposing and angular, blue just like an oversized replica of the seats at the UN General Assembly in New York. It is proudly placed atop a high base, as though waiting to be mounted by a giant, perhaps an emperor or, more appropriately for Palestine, a sphinx. It is adorned with the words 'Palestine deserves a seat'. And it is on wheels, as if ready to be wheeled to the UN to take its rightful place there.

The Chair, a replica of a seat from the UN General Assembly in New York, placed in Manarah Circle in the centre of Ramallah, waiting to be mounted by a giant, perhaps an emperor or, more appropriately for Palestine, a sphinx.

It was the sight of that chair in the Manarah, where so much has happened over the last forty-four years of occupation, that brought home to me the notion of the chair as a symbol of authority, an empty throne waiting to be assumed. What the much-heralded chair stands for is the popular acceptance of the partition of Palestine between two states, Israel and Palestine, with Palestine comprising the territories Israel occupied in 1967. But how long it has taken the Palestinian leadership to reach this point. I could not help remembering the suffering that Father endured for many years after he proposed exactly the same solution when it was a more feasible proposition, before the establishment of Jewish settlements in the West Bank. For this proposal he was accused of selling out, of treason, of betrayal. He was ostracised, condemned, and we all suffered. Father died an unhappy man, depressed after he saw what he had predicted; the rising extremism in Israel and the suffering of the Palestinian people living under a prolonged colonial occupation. But politics is not about good ideas and clairvoyance. The way it is practised here (and perhaps everywhere in the world) it is about domination and power. It is about who will sit on the empty throne.

A short distance from the chair in the Manarah is the square recently named after Yasser Arafat. He and Mahmoud Abbas, who will be taking the request for recognition of the state to the UN, were the signatories of the most shameful and damaging agreement that the Palestinians could possibly have made with Israel. But it seems they have been forgiven – all too easily forgiven.

How interesting that independence and international recognition of statehood should be expressed in the most concrete terms as winning an actual seat, represented by a blue chair, where Palestine would sit at the UN within the community of nations. Tomorrow there will be a public gathering in support of the UN bid. I saw the platform being prepared and already some cars were blowing their horns and going round and round in the tiny area of the town that is all that is left to us of Palestine's big hopes and huge ambitions. But we have the blue chair.

It seems that the settlers are planning to take their protests into Palestinian cities and villages under the banner 'Transfer the confrontations to the PA areas'. Rather than wait for the Palestinians to protest in the settlements – as if they could! – the settlers seem to be saying: let us go to them and protest against their presence on our land. So the plan is for the settlers to attack Nablus from Itamar, Ramallah from Beit El, and Hebron from Kiryat Arba.

22 SEPTEMBER

Going up to the office today I saw that the Palestinian police had redirected traffic to keep the middle of the town, the newly opened Yasser Arafat Square, not far from the Manarah where the chair proudly sits, free of cars. Along the way I saw the young men clad in *kufieh* patterned scarves with seams in the colours of the Palestinian flag.

Many cars are flying the flag. I used to hate seeing the settlers doing this during Israel's Independence Day and hoped we'd never do the same. One man had a flag coming out of his back pocket. These two nations, the Israelis and Palestinians, just love flags. When will we get over this juvenile jingoism? There is hardly any other country, except perhaps the US, that flies more flags than Israel, and we seem to be copying them.

Today the UN discusses Palestine's bid for UN recognition

of full statehood and schools are closed for the day. There is a carnival atmosphere in the streets.

But what was also clear is that the institutions of state – the police, the security forces, the Fatah-led law enforcement institutions – are trying to keep the UN initiative within limits they can control, making sure it demonstrates the popularity and support of the leadership while remaining non-violent and far from stepping on Israeli toes. So instructed our leader, who called for a 'Palestinian Spring' to accompany his UN diplomacy. How strange. The distinguishing feature of the Arab Spring has been the spontaneous uprising by civil society against the regime. In our case the regime wants to mobilise the public not to protest or to confront settlements, but rather in celebration of the leader and his party, Fatah, the besieged pillars of the Palestinian political establishment.

Meanwhile there has been an increase of over 140 per cent in the number of settler attacks resulting in Palestinian casualties and property damage compared to 2009. And what do our law enforcement authorities say to this? We have no authority in the areas where this is taking place. Areas B and C are Occupied Territories and under Israeli jurisdiction; we cannot operate there. The best we can do is to advise restraint in order to deny Israelis the excuse to strike against Palestinians. And yes, some of the local guard committees have in the past been effective, but that is not something that we ourselves can control or direct.

As the olive-picking season approaches settler violence is bound to increase. But the mobilisation of foreign volunteers to protect the farmers proceeds apace. That Palestinian farmers should need British, French and Italian volunteers to protect them as they pick olives from their own trees is a pathetic state of affairs.

A white balloon with cameras recording everything

taking place on the ground floated over the Kalandia checkpoint today, no doubt capturing every one of our movements and the faces of all the activists protesting or throwing stones at the soldiers manning the checkpoint. They use the same surveillance technique over the Haram al-Sharif. Now, as we raise flags for our hoped-for state, Israel sends cameras into the air to monitor us. As we are observed from the air we become strange and unreal to the Israelis, just as when one sees towns and villages from an aeroplane. It becomes easier to kill those you see only from a great height or distance. During the First Intifada, when Israeli soldiers injured Palestinians they allowed them to be transferred to Israeli hospitals for treatment. Now they do the killing from the air. It is so much easier and safer.

This afternoon I did a bit of gardening. The parched earth and the dry bushes, all brittle twigs, are beginning to revive with the little water I have been giving them now that autumn has begun. Already we are picking thyme, which we mix with *labneh* [our local yoghurt cheese] and oil, and I've learned how to speed up the growth of parsley by freezing the seeds before planting them. Very soon it will be time for the winter vegetables that have been nourished by the rain. It is also time to pick the olives. This year we will have a good crop.

23 SEPTEMBER

I spent the morning working in the garden and cleaning the house with Penny. She went to the celebrations while I stayed at home. They looked better on television and in any case they were staged, mainly with TV in mind.

The thought crossed my mind that I felt no loss not

being at the centre of the action, at the UN helping to draft the speech, offering ideas, helping explain things to the world. Instead I was in my house polishing the window-panes and gardening.

When the much-anticipated evening finally arrived, Penny and I dutifully sat before the television screen to hear our leader give his speech to the UN General Assembly.

So often during the speech we would experience cuts in the transmission. Abbas would start, saying, 'A state in …' then the sound and the picture would go. And Penny would shout, 'But a state where?'

It was reminiscent of Arafat's 1988 speech at the National Council declaring a Palestinian national state, when the Israelis cut off electricity and we played Scrabble by candlelight. Penny's parents were visiting us from the US and they became nervous and upset. They had come to attend our wedding, which was to take place in three days, on 18 November. I'm not sure they were all that happy for their daughter to be marrying a Palestinian committed to living in such a dangerous place.

After Netanyahu finished delivering his speech, I heard Penny calling me. She was sitting on the roof. 'Come and join me,' she said. 'There are lovely clouds in the sky.'

I grabbed a sweater, since it was already significantly cooler, and climbed up. With the noise of the television off and my eyes fixed on the sky, I relished the silence. I watched the stars shimmering and shining brightly, then dimming when the clouds drifting over veiled them. Lights from the coast shone in the distance but I didn't look at them. I looked straight up and was lost in the vastness of the universe, trying to clear my head – an essential exercise in this conflict, which I am sure will continue to plague us for many more years to come.

In the air was the promise of rain. When it comes, the summer dust will be washed away and the hardy, deep-rooted shrubs in our garden that have survived the arid summer months will come to life again.

OCTOBER 19

Went this morning to see the young man at Silwadi's, the juice shop in the centre of Ramallah, whose brother-in-law was one of the Palestinian prisoners exchanged as part of the Gilad Shalit prisoner exchange. He was smiling like I've never seen him smile. I congratulated him. He told me: 'I spoke to him this morning and was told that he was looking at the sea. My sister will be joining him tomorrow. What can I get you,' he asked.

'The usual,' I said.

I noticed that he was taking care to choose the best fruits to make the cocktail. And when I tried to pay he said no, '*Halawan* [Arabic for present]'.

I told him: 'This is the best glass of juice I have had for a long time.'

12 NOVEMBER

In the morning I arrived at the Nablus train station, a low, thick-walled stone structure, in time to board the 3:20 pm to Jerusalem. Some twenty passengers were waiting at the entrance, mostly young men and women, and a few people old enough to remember the days of train travel during the British Mandate over Palestine. The excitement was palpable: It was our chance to take a ride to Jerusalem, a city we are barred from visiting, bypassing the Israeli checkpoints along the way. As I entered the station, a porter in a dark blue uniform issued me a ticket on the Green Line. The journey would take thirty minutes, with stops planned at Hawwarah, Zatara, Uyun al Haramiya, Attarah and Kalandia – all existing checkpoints. I made my way to the waiting room. It was barren, except for low tables with brochures entitled 'Palestine Connected' showing local train networks and their destinations. Gaza. Jaffa. Haifa. Beersheba.

Soon there was an announcement in Arabic and English: the train would be arriving in three minutes. I could hear it approach, all whistles and honks. The sounds grew louder and louder until they became deafening. Then, they subsided; the train had arrived. The doors of the waiting room opened, and we were invited to step out onto Platform Number Two. The train was waiting, shrouded in rising smoke. We surged forward toward its doors as they opened for us.

But there was no getting on. The train was an image, an image projected onto a screen mounted on the far side of the wall. It was an art installation by the Palestinian artists Iyad Issa and Sahar Qawasmi, set in the pickle factory that now stands where the Nablus central station once was. This performance, marking the centenary of the station's opening, was part of 'Cities Exhibition' by the Birzeit University Museum the third edition of an annual show that allows artists to explore the social history of Palestinian cities.

After the train disappeared and the screen went blank, the fictitious passengers on the fictitious Platform Number Two were overtaken by wistful disappointment. An older man who seemed to be holding back tears lamented the passing of 'those days when we could take the train and travel freely from city to city.'

More than one hundred years ago, the Ottomans built a vast train network throughout the Middle East, first connecting Jaffa and Jerusalem and eventually linking the main cities of the Arab Middle East – Amman, Basra, Beirut, Cairo, Damascus, Jerusalem and Medina – to Istanbul. Construction on the Nablus-Jerusalem segment was interrupted by the outbreak of World War I, and the Nablus train station was largely destroyed during the Arab-Israeli war of 1948.

Today, no train crosses the borders of our tiny territory. The only Green Line we know does not connect the capitals of the Middle East; it divides them. Yet for just one moment last Saturday, the imagination of two young Palestinian artists made it possible to project ourselves beyond this dismal present.

20 NOVEMBER

Was visited by a childhood friend whose family emigrated to London just after the Israeli occupation forty-three years ago. She never came back to visit and has now lost her right (granted by Israel) to reside in the West Bank. She spent so much time thinking of Ramallah and wondering how it has changed, wanting to come for a visit but unable to face the changed reality of the place. I have been trying for years to convince her to make this trip. Now that she's come I realize that I did not enjoy having her here. For her it is more of a cemetery land, the place where members of her family are buried, where it is torturous to have missed seeing the house where she grew up and which, in the meanwhile, has been demolished and a new high building built in its place, where to enter and to leave she is stopped by Israeli soldiers. She could not relish what was good in life here or relax enough to enjoy what there is to enjoy. She was looking for a lost past that is forever gone.

194

The news about Munib Masri who was injured last Nakba Day is not good. It seems he will be crippled for life.

29 NOVEMBER

The town is full of posters about the UN General Assembly resolution 181 of 29 November 1947 partitioning Palestine into independent Arab and Jewish states with a Special International Regime for the City of Jerusalem. It appears that unlike the case for Palestinians for most Israelis this is a mystery date. A poll indicated that 73 per cent of Israeli adults do not know the historical significance of this date when the UN General Assembly decided to end the British Mandate and adopt the partition plan. Many thought that this date marked the end of the War of 1948, the Balfour Declaration and the signing of the Repatriation Agreement with West Germany. The ignorance rate was highest among the ultra-Orthodox and immigrants reaching 90 per cent and 94 per cent respectively.

28 DECEMBER

Read today that Palestinian farmers in Israel will be granted egg production quotas for the first time in the history of the state of Israel.

29 DECEMBER

Walking home today I passed the old Abu Rayya School. There in the courtyard is an almond tree. The building itself evokes painful memories. During direct Israeli rule it served as the Vehicle Licensing Department. Now it is nothing but a dirty, windswept place that merely reminds people like me who lived through the time when the Israeli military exercised full control over all civilian matters of the miseries that used to take place there, with the military authorities using their power to extract favours and torment petitioners. The one saving grace of this place is the glorious almond tree that blossoms every winter without fail. From bare branches almost black in colour, it becomes covered with celebratory white blossoms adorned with a single pink spot at the base, where the petal and stamen join. It holds on to these flimsy flowers, resisting the strong wind of the cruel month of February with its persistent rain until the blossoms turn to fruit.

As Lal Ded, the fourteenth-century Kashmiri mystic, popularly known as Lalla, wrote:

> Resilience: to stand in the path of lightning.
> Resilience: to walk when darkness falls at noon.
> Resilience: to grind yourself fine in the turning mill.
> Resilience will come to you.

Postscript

Just as I was going through the proofs of this book, Sabri Garaib died at the age of seventy-three. The very first affidavit I took for Al Haq, the human rights organisation I helped to establish, was in 1982 from Sabri. I remember sitting on the porch of his house in the village of Beit Ijza looking over the garden and the low, undulating hills planted with wheat and barley that spread out on every side. All 112 acres, I was told, were in danger of being expropriated by the new Jewish settlement of Givon Hahadasha. In the many intervening years and until his death on 18 April, Sabri repeatedly fought the settlers in order to hold on to his land. He would go to the Military Objection Committee to counter claims challenging his ownership. He would appeal to the Israeli High Court, using every recourse available. He would go to jail repeatedly for fighting off settlers who tried to stop him from farming or from removing fences they had erected. But the

Sabri, a farmer from Biet Ijza, whose name means patience. He managed to stay in his house even after the Annexation Wall separated him from most of his land and his house became surrounded on three sides by barbed wire from the nearby Jewish settlement.

settlement kept growing all around his house, claiming his land acre by acre.

So changed had the area become, and so complicated the route to Sabri's village, which is only five miles south of Ramallah, that I was not sure I would be able to find my way. I asked Shawan, the present director of Al Haq, who had more recently visited Beit Ijza, to come with me. We drove on new roads in a transformed landscape. When we got to Sabri's house in the late afternoon, I was appalled by what I saw. The house was hemmed in on three sides, with only a few yards of space left for a garden alongside a gigantic steel fence. To get to the front door, I had to pass through a metal gate that is operated from the army camp nearby and proceed down a narrow walkway lined with more steel fencing. Two cameras installed by the army monitor all movements through the gate. Sabri's family was living practically inside the Jewish settlement of Givon Hahadasha, but there were no neighbourly relations between them and the settlers.

As we sat on Sabri's porch with his sons and other guests who had come, like me, to pay their respects, I saw a settler walking his dog in the open space around his house, totally oblivious of what was taking place at his neighbour's house.

Sabri was not a man to express political views. He had inherited this land from his father and, as an only child, was determined to pass it on to his ten sons. This emboldened him, making him so formidable that I often dreaded his visits. A short stocky man with piercing dark eyes, he would force his way into my office, just as he did at any official Israeli and later Palestinian government office, and declare, 'I am Sabri and this is what I need.'

As we drove away from his house and saw how the settlements have entirely transformed the hills all around, creating a new geography of the area I used to know so well, I realized that Sabri's death marks the end of an era when it was possible to believe that the law could save Palestinian land from Jewish settlers. However, driving back to Ramallah through tunnels burrowed under the highways that connect Jewish settlements to Israel, I thought that though Israel may have won the battle of settling the West Bank, it has lost the war of making peace with its closest neighbours, the Palestinians.

A few days after that melancholy visit to Sabri's village in the centre of the West Bank, we drove to a remote windswept part of the Hebron District in the south. I used to travel quite often to the city of Hebron for work relating to my legal practice and over the years I had witnessed the distressing growth of settlements along the way, but I had never been further south than the sprawling village of Yatta. So when a friend who knew a local activist, Hafez Hereini, in the village of At-Tuwani, suggested that we go and meet him, I accepted the offer.

Driving through the two tunnels underneath Beit Jala, I was again struck by the indomitable will of the Israelis, who have dug through the hard limestone just to shorten the distance to Jerusalem and make the settlements in the south more appealing. And yet I could not help feeling that there was something desperately sad here. These settlers willingly place themselves where they are not wanted, as though it is their eternal fate not to live in harmony with the communities around them. As though this tremendous energy to gouge out the lovely hills and establish their settlements emanates from the negative persuasion that they must always force their way through and impose their presence, never trying a different approach, never hearing the numerous pleas for peace that their neighbours have repeatedly made. They seem to live with such self-hatred that they cannot believe that anyone would willingly agree to live with them.

As soon as we emerged from the dark tunnels and drove beyond the flourishing settlements near Bethlehem that had eaten up the hills on both sides of the road, I was impressed by how well tended were the low hills that the settlements had not yet claimed. Despite the fact that this is an arid to semi-arid region where a sanatorium for TB patients operated for many years, much of the land the Palestinians have been able to retain was terraced, tilled and planted with fruit trees and grapevines.

We continued past the outskirts of Halhul, Hebron and Yatta, seeing signs along the way to the numerous Jewish settlements – these, I noticed, always included writing in Arabic, as though Arabs would be allowed inside these exclusively Jewish enclaves. When we arrived at the small village of At-Tuwani, nine miles south of Hebron, with a population of 350, we parked our car by Hafez's house and went for a walk on the outskirts of the village in an area of low terraced hills to familiarise ourselves with the landscape. Every small plot was cultivated with barley or wheat and there was a number of well-maintained cisterns for collecting rainwater. As we walked along the ridges we could hear in the silence of the place the sound of the wind rustling through the patches of dry crops like undulating waves.

Right across from the low hills where we rambled was a high forested hill out of which protruded transmission towers marking the illegal outpost of Havot Maon. A number of Palestinian communities of mainly sheep farmers live on the eastern side beyond the hill in an area characterised by steep slopes where the elevation drops from 1,011 to 100 metres above sea level. Many live in the caves that are common here. In 1999 all these villages were evacuated by the Israeli army after the area was declared a live-fire exercise zone. They were allowed to return to their villages in March 2000 after the Israeli High Court issued an interim injunction permitting them to return only until it issues a final ruling – which has still not happened despite the elapse of thirteen years. We had been warned not to venture up the hill and so missed the chance of seeing the spectacular views from the steep slopes all the way down to the Dead Sea.

Though spring was coming to an early end in this arid region, we could still see some yellow marrow, a few poppies and a number of medicinal herbs with a strong fragrance that I was not familiar with from my part of the West Bank. Slowly we made our way to the house on the other side of the village where Hafez was waiting for us.

Hafez is a thin, muscular man in his late forties with kind eyes and a lined, sunburned face. Hard-working and energetic, he is under no illusions that the fight to hold on to his land and preserve the way of life of his fellow villagers in this remote region is going to be won any time soon. He is ready to take every opportunity to explain about the plight of the villagers to anyone willing to listen. He began by showing me the location of the settlements and the Palestinian villages on the map. But when he saw my confusion he said, 'Let us walk up and I'll show you how things look on the ground.'

As we walked he told me how everything they now have they've had to struggle to get. In the best Palestinian fashion, Hafez used all available means to improve the lot of his fellow villagers. 'We had no road, but the Civil

Administration would not allow us to dig one. So we had to do it at great risk and at our own expense. We convinced truck drivers from Yatta to bring the base course and the tar. This was not easy. They were worried that their vehicles would be confiscated. It had to be done at night. They piled up the loads and we decided not to wait. With our own hands we spread the material. In the morning the army came. The road was already built. "This road is illegal," they said. But it was there. It had become a fact. And the same with the water system. It was a struggle to get it connected. We still had no electricity and the Civil Administration would not allow us to connect to the grid, even though we had the transformers and cables. So when Tony Blair visited, I told him about the electricity. He got us permission. Then we built a school. Of course, we could not get a permit but we built it anyway. We had a problem getting access for the students who live in Tuba and the other villages on the eastern slope, because the settlers would not allow them to use the road.' He stopped and pointed it out. 'You see? It's over there. It runs between the forest and the settle-ment of Maon, so close to the outpost. Our problem was how to get the students to school. We needed volunteers to accompany them, like they do in the Old City of Hebron. It was not easy to convince the villagers to allow foreigners, men and women, to live in the village, but we managed it. We had two Americans who walked with the children, but the settlers from the outpost attacked them, with masks on their faces and chains in their hands. The children ran and the settlers beat up the Americans so badly they had to be hospitalised. They broke their legs. This assault was discussed in the Knesset, because it was Americans who got beaten up. From that time, it's now over six years, the army has been accompanying the kids to school. Now we have volunteers from Italy. But they are not allowed to walk the children down the hill. The Israelis don't want any more foreigners attacked. The Italians wait here, where we're standing, and watch. At the end of the school day the army takes the children back.'

As Hafez was speaking, I was thinking of what I had seen around Sabri's village in the centre of the West Bank and how, despite Sabri's singular partial success, in effect the battle there has been lost to the settlers. Formidable and determined as Sabri was, he seemed to struggle alone, whereas Hafez is waging a collective struggle. Sabri always spoke in terms of 'I', but for Hafez it is always 'we'. With their limited resources, the villagers here have not given up. Why, I wondered? Could it be that sheep farmers are simply more resilient? Or was it that the people of this region, from where marble is quarried, are living up to their reputation for being hard-headed and stubborn?

When I suggested this explanation to Hafez he did not agree. And his answer was more convincing. 'We have no choice,' he said. 'This is all we have. Where could we go?'

As I listened to this impressive, strong-willed man, I thought that the same could be said of all of us Palestinians living in the Occupied Territories. Israel might be succeeding in planting their settlements in our midst, giving the settlers the best land and the opportunity for further growth while placing limits on our spatial expansion, and yet whatever policy Israel is following, it cannot succeed, not only because of the resilience we have acquired over the many years of struggle, but because of the more simple fact that, like the farmers in the south, we too have no intention of going anywhere.

I looked straight up and was lost in the vastness of the universe, trying to clear my head – an essential exercise in this conflict, which I fear will continue to plague us for many more years to come.

ACKNOWLEDGEMENTS

The entries published here, began in the lonely recesses of my mind in the solitude of my study. There, in the early mornings and late at night I reflected on the tumultuous events happening around me and explored my thoughts, fears and emotions. But as my diary became a book, the contributions of many others in shaping, editing and preparing it for publication were crucial and most appreciated.

First I wish to thank Andrew Franklin, my friend and publisher, for his advice throughout and the superb skills he applied to the manuscript at all stages of its development. Afterwards, the manuscript passed through the able hands of my editor and friend Alex Baramki who worked tirelessly to make corrections and give advice, always encouraging, always patient and never appearing burdened when I persisted in repeating mistakes that he had already pointed out.

My thanks and appreciation go to the staff at Profile Books for all their hard work on the production and promotion of this book. In particular Penny Daniel for her

Acknowledgements

review of the manuscript, for choosing the photographs and managing the production, and Ruth Killick for her tireless work on the promotion of this and my other books. I also thank Lesley Levene for copy editing the manuscript and my literary agent Karolina Sutton of Curtis Brown for her encouragement and help. Variations of two entries, those on Nablus train station and Sabri Garaib, have been previously published in *The New York Times*.

My thanks also to Bassam Almohor for his lovely photographs of my garden and for being such a good walking companion. I also thank Emile Ashrawi and Karen Sears who provided other photographs that are published here and Yazid Anani and Vera Tamari who helped locate some of the photos from the archives. I also thank Rema Hammami who organised and accompanied me on the trip to the south of the West Bank that I write about in the postscript and her companionship.

Throughout the lengthy and engaging process of writing this book my wife, Penny, was by my side during the many travails of life under occupation described in these pages. She was always there offering advice when I needed it, reading the manuscript and commenting on the writing. But most important, she provided the much needed anchor to my precarious existence as I went through the emotional turbulence that is inevitable in writing a book of this nature.

My thanks also go to my late mother, Widad, for leaving me diaries of her youth in Jaffa, for her sense of irony, humour and storytelling skills that have inspired my writing. My late father, Aziz, left another legacy: to dare to go against the current grain and make up my own mind whatever the consequences. His vision of peace between Palestinian Arabs and Israeli Jews, which remains unrealized, has been an inspiration for me and a beacon lighting our dark existence in this conflicted region.

Raja Shehadeh
Ramallah, May 2012

Picture Credits

Al Haq 198; Bassam Almohor 94, 132, 139, 186, 205; Emile Ashrawi 62, 159, 164; Faik Tamari Family collection 55; 151; iStock 48; Karen Sears vi; Library of Congress 67; Press Association 35; Traverse Theatre Company, Edinburgh 109

While every effort has been made to contact copyright-holders of illustrations, the author and publishers would be grateful for information about any illustrations where they have been unable to trace them, and would be glad to make amendments in further editions.

Also by Raja Shehadeh
and available through
Profile Books

P

PROFILE BOOKS

PALESTINIAN WALKS

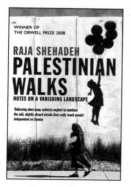

When Raja Shehadeh first started hill walking in Palestine, in the late 1970s, he was not aware that he was travelling through a vanishing landscape. These hills would have seemed familiar to Christ, until the day concrete was poured over the flora and irreversible changes were brought about by those who claim a superior love of the land.

Six walks span a period of twenty-six years, in the hills around Ramallah, in the Jerusalem wilderness and through the ravines by the Dead Sea. Each walk takes place at a different stage of Palestinian history since 1982, the first in the empty pristine hills and the last amongst the settlements and the wall. The reader senses the changing political atmosphere as well as the physical transformation of the landscape.

By recording how the land felt and looked before these calamities, Raja Shehadeh attempts to preserve, at least in words, the Palestinian natural treasures that many Palestinians will never know.

'Towards any proper understanding of history there are many small paths. I strongly suggest you walk with him' John Berger

STRANGERS IN THE HOUSE

Raja Shehadeh was born into a successful Palestinian family with a beautiful house in Jaffa, overlooking the Mediterranean. When the state of Israel was formed in 1948 the family were driven out to the provincial town of Ramallah. There Shehadeh grew up in the shadow of his father Aziz, a leading civil rights lawyer. Raja vowed not to enter a career in politics or law but inevitably did so and became an important activist himself.

In 1985 his father was killed in suspicious circumstances. The Israeli police failed to investigate the murder properly and Shehadeh, by then a lawyer, set about solving the crime that destroyed his family. In *Strangers in the House*, he recounts the painful, complex relationship he had with his father, and his frustrating, disheartening search for justice and closure. Set against the backdrop of the continuing disappearance of Shehadeh's Palestinian homeland, this is a remarkable and poignant memoir of loss that combines the personal and political to devastating effect.

'A dignified book. Shehadeh writes with great clarity and simplicity, but no bitterness about the unhappy history of his family and country.' *Independent*

A RIFT IN TIME

When Raja Shehadeh began researching his family history, he was surprised to discover a great uncle who had also been a writer at odds with the powers of the day. Najib Nassar was a journalist and romantic living in Palestine, then part of the Ottoman Empire. When he voiced his opposition to Ottoman participation in the First World War, a death sentence was put on his head. So he fled, living on the run and off the land for nearly three years.

Raja traces Najib's footsteps, travelling through the Great Rift Valley, along the Lebanese mountains and Bekaa, the Jordan Valley, the Galilee and Jordanian wilderness, he discovers that today it seems impossible to flee the cage that Palestine has become. Much of the country's history and that of its people is buried deep in the ground: whole villages have disappeared and names have been erased from the map. But now, a hundred years after Najib's escape, Raja's journey opens up a rift in time where a future free from oppression might one day be possible.

'*A Rift in Time* explores how the stability of geography and the continuity of the land have disappeared from the life of Palestinians. Piecing together a profound portrait of a territory now fragmented by numerous political borders, it offers a compelling vision both of what the land once was and of what it could be.' *Guardian*